Enjoy monogamy without monotony

Essential steps to passionate, intimate and safe lovemaking for caring couples

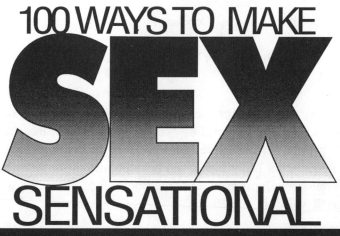

100 WAYS TO MAKE SEX SENSATIONAL

AND **100**% SAFE!

Rachel Copelan, Ph.D.

LIFETIME BOOKS, INC.
2131 Hollywood Blvd., Suite 305
Hollywood, FL 33020

Library of Congress Cataloging-in Publication Data

Copelan, Rachel.
    100 ways to make sex sensational and 100% safe! / Rachel Copelan.
        p. cm.
    ISBN 0-8119-0805-4 (paper)
    1. Man-woman relationships. 2. Sex. 3. Communication in sex. 4. Intimacy (Psychology)
    HQ801.C726   1995
    306.7--dc20   95-22778
                                                    CIP

Acknowledgment

Heartfelt thanks to the many couples, who helped
my research, by testing and proving the methods
and playful games described in this book.
These loving soulmates have receieved
the reward of: "Sexual ecstasy shared
indefinitely." It can happen
for you, too.

Editor's Statement

It is with great pleasure that Lifetime Books proudly presents *100 Ways to Make Sex Sensational and 100% Safe!* Best-selling author Rachel Copelan, Ph.D. shows us how to enjoy monogamy without monotony — safely.

I am not aware of any other book on the market that addresses *great* sex AND *safe* sex for couples who want to stay together and enjoy life with each other.

Move over Dr. Ruth! Here is a manual that applies sensitivity and compassion to increase the pleasures and benefits of a sexual relationship. It combines the best of romance, love and communication with sex.

Essential steps are provided to achieve passionate, intimate and safe lovemaking for caring couples. Safe sex can be 100 times better than changing partners 100 times.

Whether married, living together or dating, this book is for those couples looking to heighten their enjoyment together. No longer will you seek pleasure beyond each other.

Dr. Copelan has taught me — and countless others — that good sex can only happen with good love. You will find the most exciting lover is the one you are with right now. Instead of looking for variety in another person, you will enjoy unlimited variety with your one and only.

Lifetime Books hopes you and your special someone improve upon your relationship and enjoy a sexually-enhanced love life. Of course, if you are experiencing physical or mental difficulties, we strongly recommend you seek out proper medical, therapeutic or professional treatment.

Enjoy!   —   Brian Feinblum
                                               Senior Editor

Testimonial

Our Love Story

My husband and I visited Dr. Rachel Copelan for advice about getting a divorce. After fifteen years of routine sex, we were kind of bored with each other and fighting about every little thing.

After we returned home from counseling, we decided to give the relationship one more try because of the children. It's been a couple of months now since we started using Dr. Copelan's new approach. We are more romantic now and enjoy at least a half hour of outercourse before intercourse. We also play the games at least once a week. We feel like kids again.

Sex has become better than it was when we first fell in love, because I get into it, instead of leaving it up to him. We have discovered so much about each other, it's like being with a new person. We are at the point where we use all of our senses and now I can accept looking and listening and acting sexy, which used to embarass me before.

The best news is, instead of breaking-up we are making-up.

Passionately,

Carol and Philip

Table of Contents

Preface

Sexual intimacy has always had its hazards. However, with the advent of AIDS these hazards have become life threatening and demand re-thinking of our sexual mores. Monogamy and knowing your sexual partner has become crucially important. Self-discipline and restraint may save your life as well as prevent prolonged, agonizing suffering. It therefore becomes important to know as much as possible about safe sex and love and how to manage it in your life.

The basic instincts of sex and love are too powerful and universal to ignore. Sex is nature's lusting for existence. Without it life does not develop and perpetuate itself. The generic pool is preserved and passed on by sex. Nature makes sure that this process continues. Nature assures that the life force continue to manifest and is more interested in protecting the genetic pool than in love. Therein lies one of the origins and reasons for passion and fantasy. It makes things happen that wouldn't without it!

Sex is a great motivator and is the cement which bonds relationships. It can enslave, destroy or elevate. This force is an amoral one which humans have to channel to serve cultural ends. It can be sacrementalized and be a major pathway to spiritual development. It can also degrade and be a major instrument of seduction and betrayal. As the philosopher theologian Tillich stated - "power is never good except to be good who uses it."

Behavior without responsibility is license. Taking responsibility for everything we do, say, and think improves our self-concept and self-esteem. Sex can thus be an instrument of deception or communicative intimacy.

In this regard, let me state two principles which I would advise you to keep in mind at all times:

1. *All mental illness has an element of communicative deception.*
2. *All mental healing has an element of communicative intimacy.*

We are happiest with people with whom we can have communicative intimacy. It gives us a sense of connection, security, containment, and sharing and caring and helps us fulfill our fullest potential. *This is the reason that friendship is the best basis for a successful lasting marriage.* People with this type of relationship live longer, have less illness, more energy, and achieve more of their highest potential. They are happier and thus are kinder to themselves and others. People who are unhappy with themselves usually have a pool of unconscious rage which often converts itself into hurting others and acting out in destructive manners such as criminal behavior, domestic abuse, and a large variety of jealousy and scapegoating.

Present day circumstances mandate that *safe sex must be practiced.* Moments of passion where reason is abdicated are too dangerous. It is no longer safe to indulge in transitory satisfactions without regard to future consequences.

The Dionysian must be tempered with the Appolonion. Head and heart must be balanced. The feelings give us passion, sensitivity, connection, and a feeling of containment. However, when the analytical intellect is abandoned feelings can run amok and be brutal and devastating. The intellect gives clarity, direction and understanding. However, it can also be aloof, cruel, and impersonal.

The problems of AIDS is causing an evolutionary advance necessitating advances in discipline and mastery and a deeper development of loving, caring and sharing. Problems are opportunities and demands to grow. Whereas they are destructive if overwhelming, there is no growth without problem-solving. Realizing this, we can develop a positive attitude and approach which moves us forward and upward to higher growth and integration. All life seeks to realize itself and fulfill its potential. Understanding this and developing understanding and wisdom is the safest, most constructive, and most fulfilling way to go. Simplistic answers do not do the job and are hazardous.

I would like to close by speaking about love. We may not be able to define it, however, we surely know when we experience it. Life should be a creative, passionate exploration of love and a celebration of the mystery of life. Everything has potential meaning which you must constellate to serve your uniqueness. Assuming that you are a person of good will with a commitment to sharing and caring, my injunction would be: "Get everything, but don't let anything get you!" Enjoy the voyage. Enjoy Dr. Rachel Copelan's amusing and informative book, *100 WAYS TO MAKE SEX SENSATIONAL and 100 Percent Safe.*

Dr. Harry Seagal, medical psychiatrist, is in private practice (since 1969) in Bel Air and Beverly Hills, California. He is a member of The American Psychiatric Society, served as President-elect of Group Psychotherapy Association and taught Physiological Psychology in Antioch University, Venice, California.

Foreword

From Dr. David Neff, Hollywood chiropractor to the stars.

I am always pleased to refer my patients to Dr. Rachel Copelan, when they complain of problems relating to their sexual function. I believe she is the best in the business.

Her methods are not only traditionally sound but also inventive and focus on holistic solutions, involving the mind and spirit. The feedback I receive from my patients has always been positive.

Her new book, *100 Ways to Make Sex Sensational and 100% Safe*, answers the need for people to know how to enjoy intimacy without risk. There is a growing emergency for this information to reach the millions of couples who are in need of help. She presents a way for them to improve in the privacy of their homes instead of visiting a therapist.

I am happy to recommend the book.

Introduction

Dr. Rachel Copelan

Promiscuous sexual behavior has resulted in a life-or-death crisis for the entire human population. Right now, *one out of six people is infected with a venereal disease.* That includes AIDS and 28 other sexually transmitted ailments. If the trend continues at the present pace, *by the year 2000, the figures will be doubled and increase to one out of three people.*

When careless lovers have intercourse, they are exchanging bodily fluids with everybody they've had sex with during the prior ten years. What's the solution to this world-wide dilemma? The answer is twofold:

One— Take a blood test. There are clinics in most major cities. There is usually no waiting and you receive test results in about 24 hours. The cost is about 50 dollars.

Two— Instead of seeking variety by sleeping-around, we need to add variety inside a monogamous relationship, where there's good health and trust.

There will be no cheating when your partner discovers you are the greatest. That's what you can become by practicing the program outlined in this book. About half of all marriages, begun in happiness, end in break-ups. No one has ever taught us how to enhance sexual pleasure and make love last. We hear about the problems, rather than the solutions. Lovers who no longer feel the passion, turn away from each other. Changing partners doesn't change the problem.

For many, marriage has become less endearing, and more of an endurance contest. Sex has a three-fold purpose. Beyond recreation and procreation, it can be a sacrament of unity. When all three needs are fulfilled, it presages lifelong happiness in a stable, enduring marriage which respects the dignity of human life. Long-term alliances can become better with time. We need to be more adventurous and eliminate the boredom.

Monogamy without monotony can curb the spread of ravaging disease and put an end to the catastrophe of broken homes, economic disaster and the shattered lives of millions of displaced children. Sexual ignorance and dysfunction have battered traditional family values. Long-term lovers do not have to settle for short-term passion. Longevity of intimacy can be accomplished with self training. Men can command potency and women can improve their natural hormonal secretions.

The magic and mystery of long-lasting soul-mating, is that two people, coming from different backgrounds and values, become so intertwined and sensitive to each other's needs, that they are content for the rest of their lives to have no other lover but their "one and only." What a wondrous state of being!

You can share their secrets and become whatever your mind and spirit will allow. The saddest thing is when two people, who have loved each other passionately, become disenchanted, and behave like hostile strangers. They may be sitting across from each other at the breakfast table with minds and hearts miles apart. Each one may feel injured and hopeless and blame the other. If you have a significant other, cherish the joy and nourish the love.

If you don't have a "one and only" and are still searching to find that certain somebody, there is a safe solution. It's enjoying *Outercourse* before risking *Intercourse*. You'll find safe sex can be so thrilling, you'll be happy to trade musical beds for mutual fidelity.

Chapter 1

"Outercourse"- Safest Sex In The World

☑ *How to attract the right person*
☑ *Dating, relating and serious mating*
☑ *Certain words that turn up the heat*
☑ *Slow-motion increases sensuality*

 Sexual fulfillment is a powerful factor in human happiness. Beyond mere biological satisfaction, spiritual ecstasy is within the grasp of every mature person, who is both sensuous and adventurous. Single people should be cautious because these days sleeping-around is risky. Yet, intimacy can be 100% safe and also super sensational from the first date to the long-time mate. The difference between dangerous intercourse and safe-sex is making love leisurely, without being goal oriented. For decades the emphasis has been on achieving the big "O." Straining to reach orgasm has taken away much of the sensate focus on pure pleasure in the moment. We have become so intent on climaxing, that our sensory responses are diminished. The mind feeds upon the stimulation of all five senses.

This is especially important when meeting a new person, as we receive impressions, our mind sorts them out and determines whether this will be a future relationship. It's a matter of life and death that people take the time to know each other. Sex with love and commitment is worth waiting for. Too many give up the search and live out their entire lives having sex with strangers. This behavior no longer is appropriate. We live in a threatening world where we cannot dive into sexual relationships without rational thinking. While sex is best when it's playful and spontaneous, it also needs to be thoughtful. Spontaneity will blossom later after you know more about a person.

Pleasure Without Penetration

The safest pathway to great sexual intimacy, is to practice Outercourse before attempting Intercourse. That means you give up playing the field carelessly, and focus on really getting to know one person in the deepest sense. Outercourse is basically *slow-motion foreplay and can last for hours*. Intercourse is the instinctive drive for penetration and presupposes there will be an exchange of bodily fluids, which is the dangerous part of lovemaking. Once two people find they are well mated, they can continue the sensuous outercourse over a period of time, until both are sure of each other's intentions and know they are physically healthy. Until you receive results of blood tests, outercourse is the safest way to make love.

There is a consensus of female opinion that men tend to rush sex, often cutting off a budding relationship before it fully blooms. Start warming each other up on a slow burner and you'll both reach full heat without strain or struggle. The longer you simmer, the hotter it gets. This book presents hundreds of ways to take the monotony out of monogamy once you have given up the search for a partner and are ready to stick to one lover.

When we slow down we are able to fully savor the pleasure of our senses. This method of lovemaking assures that you will really know a lot about each other well in advance of taking chances. By the time passion is consummated with intercourse, lovers will probably be ready to give up the game of changing partners and stick to one mate. Even married people can remain strangers if they lack the ability to communicate and trust. Poor souls, they will never know what they're missing unless they reach out and learn how to make the most of their natural assets. Techniques as described in this book, will ensure that single or married, you need never get bored with the same person. With slow-motion outercourse it will just get better and better with time.

Helping Women Become Fulfilled

When lovemaking is primarily outercourse it should be leisurely and last from 30 minutes to several hours. The length of time depends on the circumstances. Most women respond better to a slower pace. Here are three magical statements which will help any woman relax and increase her sensations of pleasure:

> *1. "We've got plenty of time."*
> *2. "I enjoy giving you pleasure."*
> *3. "Tell me what you want me to do."*

His attitude releases her from the pressure so many men place upon women when they are in a hurry to insert. The act of intercourse is the culmination of the act of outercourse. It usually leads to climaxing, which ends the encounter. It does not require as much creativity as outercourse, with its unlimited possibilities for variation. I'm not suggesting that lovers never penetrate. Full intercourse will be wonderful later, when they have proved themselves an important part of each other's life. What I am suggesting is that people take time until they know the attraction is deeper than physical. The object is: "falling in love" not "falling in sex."

Outercourse is a process that lets you know more about each other. And the more you know, the more there is to love about each other. Without knowing ourselves and the inner world of our mate, we can never be content with one partner, nor adapt and live in harmony with the world around us. Outercourse is the most pleasurable, safe alternative to intercourse for singles who have not yet found that special person. It is the way to enjoy great sexual intimacy without risk. It's sensual. Leisurely. Relaxed. *And without the exchange of body fluids*. There's less puffing and huffing and a lot more laughing and loving.

Outercourse is a feast of the senses. It's talking, selecting words that enable instead of disable. Tender touching and stroking can lead to erotic massage. Bathing together and exploring each of the many wonders of the other's body.

Outercourse lovemaking eliminates fear of penetration, pregnancy and disease, and allows the couple to get to know each other without pressure. Women have always said that they like men who take their time. They know that time builds trust and makes for greater fulfillment for both of them. This is because feeling comfortable with a partner reduces anxieties and allows for freedom of exploration.

Outercourse doesn't mean you have to avoid intercourse forever. When you select your mate and intimacy is exclusive for three months, both parties should take a blood test, together. They can then check on each other's results. If they are both free from communicable disease and still care about each other, they can feel comparatively safe about genital contact and completing the sexual process. If they cannot wait, they can arouse each other with outercourse and climax using a condom or masturbation.

Dating with Mating in Mind

If you seem to have trouble attracting that one-and-only, here are some tips on the art of making the first move. If you are female and wait to be selected, you will have to take what comes your way. In the past men were expected to make the approach while the woman sat back and waited. If he turned out to be a loser or a "dork," she blamed him for being who he was to begin with. And, strangely, she kept attracting the same unwanted types again and again. These days women have the option to be selective. The dichotomy between male and female roles in courtship is blurred.

How do you let a person know you feel an attraction, without seeming too eager? Whether you are male or female, showing genuine interest in the other person is always a safe and sensible way to get started. I asked a number of single people which kind of approach received their best response. Here's what several of them said:

"A compliment about the appearance of my hair, when it looked terrible, made me smile."

"Her humor got my attention. I moved closer when I heard people near her laughing."

"He piqued my interest when he asked me how does a guy like him get to know someone like me."

"She was poised and confident. She looked me straight in the eyes."

The best approach to a new possible mate is to behave like an artist when he approaches a canvas. Use creative imagination, artistic skill and sensitivity. Don't be dull. Be colorful. Your objective is to develop rapport and open up personal conversation. Communication is the first step toward safe sex. It's important to find out as much as possible about the other person, so that you can develop a friendship before getting physical. Anything you can do with a stranger feels much better with a friend. An added advantage to leisurely outercourse is that lovers become skilled at control while arousing each other. Selfish behavior is lessened. There is patience instead of pressure. The sense of urgency is set aside. Instead of rushing to the act of sex, we live in the moment and feel greater intensity.

Postponement of intercourse adds to the excitement of future promise. Waiting for the blood tests to come back (negative) sparks passion and patience.

To attract the right person here's some advice: Remember that first impressions affect the future. How you dress, your voice, your confidence all contribute to the picture, viewed by a new prospect. So, put your best foot forward. You can show your warts later, when you have grown fond of each other. By that time, it won't matter. Nobody's perfect and when you confess vulnerability you become more lovable, more real. Assume it's going to work out into a worthwhile friendship, at least.

Become not only charming, but disarming, by asking questions. In a recent study, it was found that people are more comfortable with a mate they have things in common with, such as: age, social customs, preferences in cultural areas, similarity in education and family background. While there are many uniquely personal requirements in selecting a mate, there are also some general truths which apply to all of us.

Five Things That Should be Checked Out

Before trusting body, emotions and spirit to another person, make sure this will be a good experience for you. Better safe, than sorrow, later. In the case of AIDS it can be too late. At one time sex was an overpowering motivation. Now, priorities have shifted and self-preservation heads the list.

1. **Physical Health.** In addition to assuring each other that they are free from venereal disease, people should be in reasonably good shape. They should exercise, eat sensibly and have good hygiene habits and live up to their highest potential in attractiveness. This is especially true at the beginning of a relationship. Later on we tend to become complacent, less aware of a mate's appearance. "I've grown accustomed to your face, etc" is the way it goes. (Don't expect a mate to be in perfect shape, if you're not.)

2. **Emotional Honesty.** Be real! Honest people communicate feelings, not just words. Sooner or later, the truth will come out, so open up and tell it like it is. If you're a male and feel hurt, don't be afraid to show it. If you are a female and get annoyed at his behavior, let him know. We must not be afraid of reversing personality roles because this is the surest way to reach and teach the other person how you feel. Negative thoughts, fears from past experiences, or hidden wounds intrude on the free exchange of feeling.

3. **Romantic Affection.** Openly demonstrate signs of caring. Don't be stingy with your good strokes. It is just as important for establishing love as sexual intercourse; for some people, even more so. Men need tenderness as much as women. Lack of

outward affection is a primary source of disillusion and breakups. Traditionally, manly men were not expected to show feelings of sensitivity. However, today's women demand this quality. By the same standard, women should be more giving to men. Buy men gifts or treat them to dinner. Do all the romantic things women expect from men. Why not? It's about time. Giving is a sign of strength on the part of the giver, and makes love stronger and last longer.

4. **Playful and Funny.** Humor is the glue that keeps a relationship from falling apart even when there are differences. People relish the company of those who make them laugh. Having fun together enhances intimacy and reduces performance anxiety. It's more than merely the laughter. Humor represents a coping attitude expressed toward life, in general. In a subtle way, humor touches deeper values that you both can share. Notice what your partner laughs about. See if you think it's funny. Above all, humor accentuates the positive and helps eliminate the negative baggage that we all carry around from previous relationships.

5. **Sexual Attraction.** A large part of erotic magnetism is chemistry. Our bodily juices flow when we confront certain types. We've heard about 'Love at first sight.' Sex at first sight, is probably closer to the truth. Sex affairs often turn out to be only one-night-stands if they are merely based on physical chemistry. For most of us, when the passion is satisfied, we want something deeper. Good lovers need mind and emotions to become great. However, few ever achieve their potential, because they settle for less than they could get.

Women, much more than men, carry into a relationship problems linked to unpleasant sexual experiences from childhood and adolescence. Surveys point to a disturbing fact, that almost half of all women have been sexually molested as children, abused as adults — or both. Growing up in dysfunctional homes is responsible for six out of eight relationships breaking up. It acts like a self-fulfilling prophecy. If either of you grew up with a lack of affection, the early deprivation will affect both of you. Learning about yourself requires that you look back and ferret out the roots of self-defeating behavior. Looking back into your past need not be painful if you realize that a backward glance will give you the necessary insight to move forward more speedily.

Knowledge brings with it the illumination of the causes which hamper our development into sexual maturity. Once this information is examined rationally in the light of its usefulness for progress, a person can take giant steps forward. It is not necessary to actually live through each unresolved period of childhood and adolescence. Gaining awareness can help you to take giant steps into the level that brings the greatest fulfillment.

We have all encountered people, who, as adults in body only, continue to behave in a childish manner where the opposite sex is concerned. It's difficult for some to admit the pain they suffered in childhood. It does not make us less lovable. In fact, sharing pain draws caring people closer. Some men fear loss of respect in showing their vulnerability. Instead, two people can help each other feel secure and strong.

I recall a couple who were talking divorce. He broke down as he told of his miserable childhood. She put her arms around him and said: "I love and respect you even more for the pain and suffering that you had to endure."

Questions Reveal What We Conceal

If you have problems in getting close and a reluctance toward commitment, discover why. To understand yourself and to prepare to put the past behind you, ask yourself a few questions:

1. When did my problem start?
2. How was my sexual development interfered with?
3. What were my parents' attitudes toward sex?
4. Did a special incident occur that shocked me?
5. What sort of sex education did I receive?

6. What was the source of my sex knowledge?
   From family?... From school?... From friends?
7. How did the various explanations differ?
8. Were my parents interested and sympathetic toward my sexual growth?

Keep in mind that you must discover who you are before you are ready for the exchange of passionate interaction. However, before you can have great sex, you need to find a great partner. To catch up with the elusive mate of your dreams, you need a plan. We use maps to find destinations, yet most people look for love in all the wrong places. So many people end up fumbling in the dark with someone they know little about and break-up is inevitable. Some people even get married to strangers before they have had a chance to really get to know them.

First, make up your mind about the qualities you want in a mate as well as the traits that are intolerable.

Partners should observe the following rules of fairness:

1. I am open to the needs of my partner.
2. I am clean, well-groomed and attractive.
3. I show emotions and communicate feeling.
4. I enjoy participating in new techniques.
5. I am demonstrative and act romantic.
6. I compliment my mate's lovemaking skills.
7. I'm willing to release old inhibitions.

Why Men Select Certain Types of Women

Individual men usually relate to the looks of women in his family. Part of the magic is that the man enjoys the feeling of comfort that comes with what's familiar. It's what he's used to. Some men like their women tall, some prefer small, thick or thin. Others respond to a host of variations in between. Thank goodness, because this variation in taste assures every woman that some man will find her intriguing.

In a study done among single men of all ages, they had one thing in common. *Facial expression* topped the list of items men found important when they first see a new woman. Notice we are not talking about facial beauty, rather the personality that emanates from within. Once a man likes the face, his eyes will wander over the entire person. Next, they love women who speak with their eloquent eyes. We've all heard the adage, "Eyes are the mirrors of the soul." This has proven true where body language is concerned.

In olden times, coquettes enticed men with fluttering eyelids that sent a message of innocence. For some men that still works. Most men are seduced easily by women who slowly lower their eyelids when they look at a man. It connotes deep emotional feeling.

The use of a woman's slow, over the shoulder glance, has won over many a reluctant bachelor. Adventurous men love to discover the mystique behind a woman's eyes. Half-closed lids are called "bedroom eyes," because of their erotic mystery. An eye movement to avoid is the quick blink, which is considered a way of shutting off the other person from entering your mind or heart.

Why Women Select Certain Types of Men

The male's body-language can be a turn-on or turn-off. A man says things with his body movements that he might not say in words. His walk, his hand gestures, the body posture and the tone of his voice all reveal his intentions. This selection process goes on at a subliminal level and connects to the woman's past experiences. If the sum total delivers a message that is positive, above all trustworthy, a woman will allow him to move in closer. If a man's body language is threatening, she moves away, in the opposite direction, unless she's masochistic.

What does your body language say? Does it appeal or repel? Body language refers to gender signals that both men and women send to each other through facial expression and physical movements. We send signals with more than the words that we speak. Your body signals have more sex appeal than spoken words because they come from your subliminal mind where your real feelings are stored. Men are charmed by a woman who speaks with her body movements. And women reject men who do not stand up to their inherent potential. It shows in his posture.

Body talk presents subtle messages. The simplest non-verbal message is the head nod. Moving the head up and down ever so slightly, lets a man know that you are agreeable to his thoughts and desires. The negative head shake does the opposite. This usually happens without people realizing they are doing so.

Your hands also do a lot of talking. Hands let others know how you feel about getting closer. The common handshake sends a message of strength or weakness. The clenched fist represents anger and so forth.

Here are some handy "no-nos" that turn people off:

Don't fold or cross your arms. This says you are afraid of becoming involved.

Avoid clasping your hands together. This means you are tense, that you need to unwind before you are receptive.

Keep your hands away from your face or hair. This says you are unsure about your appearance, that you are anxious and lack confidence.

Don't fiddle with keys or any other object. This shows restlessness; that you are not living in the moment.

The best female hand language is to confidently touch his hands and let him feel your relaxed vibrations. He will be more likely to put his life in your hands when he trusts your touch. A woman who welcomes a man into her life greets him not only with open arms but with relaxed hands and wrists. The movements of her hands show kindness and gracefulness.

You can also watch *his* hand language and discover how he feels about you. *Here are some clues:*

Showing the palm of the hand is associated with courtship. The man "offers his hand," offering his love in marriage. The man who shows his palm to a woman is saying I can be trusted to care for you. You know you have attracted a man with the right body language when he moves his shoulders toward you, and face-to-face, looks into your eyes.

Advice to Men

To reach a deep level of trust, ask her questions about herself. She will sense that you are interested in her as a person, not just as a bed companion. Ask her to share secrets from her childhood. Exchange memories of your own. Find similarities. Symbiotic memories become strings that bind people to each other. Compare early lovemaking experiences. What was she first told about sexual differences? What were her fears? When two people meet for the first time, the most impressive thing to say is "Tell Me About Yourself." You'll do well with this. It's probably the favorite topic of the greatest number of people.

Tips for Single Men and Women

Be poised. Let your body language send a message of self-esteem. Don't act insecure. Nobody wants a loser.

Show signs of encouragement. Learn to smile more. Don't complain about other dates or spouses. Be complimentary.

Be a good listener. Everybody needs a good friend. Love that begins with friendship is destined to be long-term.

Freely compliment. Find some good qualities and call attention to something he/she is proud of.

Hugging tells a lot. You will know, by the feel if this will lead to total body contact later on.

Advice to Women

In interviewing hundreds of men, I have discovered that they are often shy about making the initial approach to a woman they really like. Fear of rejection is the single man's number one problem. Even a not-so-attractive woman can have the man of her choice if she is willing to reverse gender-role behavior. In the past women were expected to be the receiver of attention, rather than the giver. If holding back seems preferable to you, consider this: Assertive women tend to have more men in their lives. They don't wait for things to happen. They make things happen!

A Warm Voice Says it All

Once a person takes a good look at a possible mate and likes what he/she sees, then the sound of the voice can make or break the visual impact. It helps to listen to your own voice on a recorder. Practice adding warmth and charisma. Check the sound to determine if it's too high, or too low, too fast, or too slow. People tell me that they run the other way from even the most attractive person whose voice is irritating, harsh or whiny. Fortunately, voices can be retrained to be charismatic and soothing to the ear. Talk into an audio recorder and then listen to the way you sound. Try variations and improvements. It's worth the effort.

Give Sex the Time it Deserves

People spend hours doing mundane things like going to shows, cooking, eating, exercising, watching television, yet when it comes to sex, they tend to rush through it in a few minutes. According to a recently published major survey, *Sex In America*, published by Little, Brown,  couples take between 15 minutes and one hour to make love. The average is somewhere around one half-hour. It's worth taking time to develop great lovemaking skills, especially when couples are getting to know each other.

It's even more important if the relationship is having difficulties surviving differences. Often, taking more time to be intimate will save the union. When people give up and break up they take their problems with them into the next relationship.

Women have always wanted more leisurely preliminaries. The time is past when a women will allow a man to indulge in intercourse without the necessary preliminaries. Let's talk about the fine art of intimacy. For *foreplay* to be effective a certain mood has to be established. This is true for both men and women. We must feel comfortable physically in the presence of the other person. Because a man is usually larger and stronger than a woman, he must make a special effort to help her relax and trust him fully, before making love to her. Only when a woman feels comfortably relaxed will her sexual machinery respond to his touch.

Trusting a man is paramount to the degree of pleasure she enjoys when he touches her body. The gentle, tender lover is prized by all women. The strong drive for penetration should only be manifested by him when she shows readiness and desire. Sex that happens too fast doesn't allow time for people to develop strong roots. Take at least twice the time you normally would for foreplay. Really drag it out. If you usually spend a half-hour, make it an hour and a half. Slow sex presupposes that the man has learned to control his sexual reaction. If not, this book has several proven methods described in subsequent chapters. Any man can help himself in the correction of his erection. We are assuming that his problem is not organic; that he has checked out his organs and glandular function with a doctor.

Outercourse lovemaking does not have to lead to a climax. As long as it feels good, stay with the erotic sensual pleasure. This is the best way I know to eliminate performance anxiety. Outercourse instead of intercourse involves lots of body hugging and kissing.

After a man invites a woman out, she can make things happen faster in the privacy of her own home. An intimate setting is conducive to getting closer. Men are excited by women who offer them a view of a cozier kind of home life than the one they are experiencing. Most single men, even in the upper income bracket do not eat well, or live as healthy a life as men who have a woman in their lives. That's why married men outlive the single ones by about ten years. *Monogamy ensures longevity.* That's an important fact for women to tell men who avoid commitment. It will give her points toward settling him down to a better way of life. Men find women who take an interest in their well-being, irresistible and highly desirable.

The most romantic gesture a single woman can make is treating her man to a home cooked dinner, especially if she is a career person. Yes, the way to a man's heart is still through his stomach. That's how he grew to love his mother; she nourished him. Made him feel wanted. And yes, men love to be babied by women they feel attracted to. That's why they are so obsessed with women's breasts.

Candlelight and wine, on a well-set table with flowers, warms any bachelor's heart. And, if he's worth the effort, this will lead to his being more generous when he invites you out. If you don't have the proper setting, take him out to an intimate restaurant. In a recent poll, 55% of men listed this as their number one preference on how women can show them affection.

A house date is a great way to begin a close relationship, because it offers the ambiance to have intimate conversation. Discover in advance the likes and dislikes as to food preferences. A magical question that people love to be asked is: *"What are you most interested in?"* Before spending time with a person, learn about those things he/she is involved in. Men and women are both extremely attracted to people who share their concerns and pastimes.

Ask about the person's family. Don't interrupt to talk about your own until it is appropriate. Show genuine caring and sympathy. This is very endearing to the unattached person who may not have anyone to open up with. Don't be afraid to express interest. This can be done without coming on too strong. If you are emotionally open and giving, your companion will reciprocate. If not, something is wrong and the sooner you find out, the better, so you can get on with your life.

Women should show that they have a great capacity for giving and receiving pleasure. Men love to be admired as much as women do. Every man hopes women find him attractive. There appears to be a biological improvement in erotic pleasure for the woman who is assertive in her approach to men. Her own sexual pleasure actually increases as she acts more aggressive toward the male.

Men love to spend time with women who are self-starters. If you are able to show him that you enjoy life, in every way, that you are intrinsically a happy person, you are well on your way toward making him a permanent fixture in your life.

Men want to latch on to a woman who is already happy before they come into her life. No man wants the burden of a depressed female who needs him to perk up her spirits. This is not his responsibility. This is hers. Happy women always have men chasing after them. Men love to bask in the aura of a woman's joyfulness. They probably didn't get enough of it as children.

High on the list of requirements that men find important in the women they admire is a *robust sense of humor*. A rib-tickling laugh makes a good date even better, and a bad date tolerable! When you look, sound, smell, touch and taste right — and then turn out to be an amusing person, you've got it made. I suggest you learn at least one funny joke to break the ice when conversations lag. If the jokes are a little raunchy, men feel even better about you. You have eliminated their fear of spending time with a prude, which they tell me is the worst possible scenario they can experience with a new woman.

Ten Things Men Like Most in Women

1. **She says what she wants without being critical.** Don't complain during or after lovemaking. He wants you to tell him in advance, how he can satisfy you. The worst nightmare for a man is to make love to a woman, do the best he knows how and then find out she is frustrated and dissatisfied with his lovemaking.

2. **She is amorous and likes to please him.** Positive reinforcement of his efforts is high on the list. Men like a hint that you are feeling amorous. Some assertiveness is appreciated. Don't wait for him to make all the advances. Start the foreplay on your own and he'll take over.

3. **She enjoys being playful spontaneously.** How about playing footsies under the table in restaurants? Men love sneaky love games. Especially when other people are around. Patting him on the booty or resting her hand on his thigh under the tablecloth, excites the adventurous male.

4. **She smiles when he looks at other women.** Don't behave like a jealous woman. Men who enjoy looking at other women often do so to compare them with the one they have selected. As long as you know he returns to you, why not play along? No one wants to be treated like a prisoner. Acting self-assured is very sexy.

5. **She should have her own life and be emotionally strong.** There was a time when men preferred weak, weepy women. It made them feel more macho. Times have changed. Men in the 90's want gutsy women who meet them half-way in a 50-50 relationship. Airheads who get by as ornamental sex objects are out in the '90's. However, men don't want to play second fiddle to your career. So, go for a balanced life and you'll get a harmonious relationship.

6. **She should be easy-going about neatness.** In other words, if he wants to throw his things around sometimes, he doesn't want to be nagged about it. Men avoid women who are too orderly, because they don't want to change their lifestyles too much to accommodate her. However, they prefer that she be neat and orderly in her own personal habits. If you see a contradiction and an inequality of gender, you are right. Men want it both ways.

7. **She's ready to go places on the spur of the moment.** Men prefer women who get dressed quickly and are willing to go to sports events without making a big deal about it. They say women spend too much time putting on make-up and getting dressed. They hate being kept waiting. This is O.K. for very special occasions but they rebel when it is a steady habit. Men say this is the main reason why they enjoy going out with male friends. They make do the way they are dressed at the moment.

8. **She should be reliable and be on time.** Men complain about women who are late for appointments. They prefer us to be more predictable and less flighty in our attitudes. Where money is concerned men wish women would spend less on clothes and trivia. They feel this way even if a woman is earning her own money. They would like women to be more like men, except in the bedroom.

9. **She should be more lustful during sex.** While men are sometimes in a romantic mood, they enjoy a woman who does not need to be romanced every time he feels steamy. To the woman, intimacy means doing and saying things romantically. With the man, his feelings are more overtly physical and he doesn't always want to communicate on a higher level. Most women want a love base to their sexuality, compared to a small percentage of men.

10. **She should enjoy sharing his erotic fantasies.** Assuming his fantasies are compatible with hers, a wanted woman can listen to erotic, sensual thoughts of her mate without feeling insulted, even if the fantasy doesn't always include her. She should join into the fun of the moment and add her own images to the shared fantasy. When a man can share his fantasies, he doesn't need to look elsewhere for gratification. Instead of acting out, he plays mind games with his number one love-mate. This gratifies his need for variety in a safe way.

Where to Look for Mr. or Mrs. Right

Meeting your ideal mate requires some thought. If you're looking for an intellectual type, take some courses on subjects that interest you. Then, you will surely have something in common with the person you meet there, beyond the physical attraction. If you're a sports lover, try a sports club or run a marathon. Go to the right place to find the right person. In this way you can assure yourself you will have something in common with him/her.

First impressions affect the future. How you dress, the sound of your voice, and the display of your confidence, all contribute to the picture viewed by a new date. No matter how liberated women have become, they still say they need to be romanced before they feel intimate. There is a consensus of female opinion that men tend to rush sex, and by so doing cut off a budding relationship before it blooms. Women tell me they like to take their time, and get to know their partners. Time builds trust and makes for greater fulfillment for both men and women. When there's lots of time for outercourse, intercourse becomes more meaningful.

The Taste of Love

Seduction usually begins with the taste buds. Food is offered, or a drink. The very first time a man offers to feed a woman, he is doing something more than just buying her dinner. He is enticing her through her sense of taste to get closer to him, for our sense of taste is fundamentally sexual. The mouth is connected to showing love in many ways. Sharing food. Smiling at each other. The sound of the voice flowing through the lips. And the message it sends through kissing.

The First Kiss — A Determining Factor

It can awaken desire for intimacy, or turn a woman away, completely repulsed. Women prefer the first few kisses to be affectionate rather than extremely sexual. This is the kind of rapport that makes a woman trust a man for more serious kissing later on. A first kiss should intrigue a woman, not frighten or turn her off. How you kiss can be the beginning of a lifetime of love or the beginning of the end. Women talk about the way they don't like to be kissed but seldom about the way they enjoy kissing. People need to know how to initiate kissing from the very beginning of a match. Relationships that start with friendly cheek kissing usually outlast those that begin with passionate tongue-in-mouth. Soul-kissing, is reserved for later in the relationship. Check the last chapter on "Spiritual Intercourse."

How To Become A Skilled Kisser

If a kiss is prolonged and unhurried, it can help a woman reach new and constantly heightened plateaus of pleasure. There is no place that should be considered out of bounds for a one-and-only lover, to kiss. A clean, healthy body is entirely lovable and kissable. Reluctance to accept a loved one's body totally is a sign of a problem on the part of the reluctant one. However, where and what one kisses during outercourse is an entirely personal thing and there should be no anxiety about whether one or another kind of kissing is normal or not. Everything is normal if it meets with the approval of both people concerned. Always inform before you perform.

Whatever one's preference may be, the fact remains that kissing is an essential part of the foreplay leading to satisfactory sex for women. It sets the stage for what is to follow, by giving a woman confidence in her desirability as well as effectively stimulating her sensory reflexes.

When lips cherish with full reciprocal acceptance, the level of feeling can rise to a spiritual communion between two lovers, above and beyond mere sexual union.

Kissing is a builder of understanding on a more profound level than words are capable of. The lips and tongue not only taste, but they are super-sensitive to touch and the reception of the most subtle vibrations of thought.

How Kissing Turns You On

Recent research involving the body's chemnical reaction to kissing, revealed some remarkable results. Why does it excite us? The survey showed that both men and women react with increased blood pressure, heightened circulation, quickening of pulse, and deeper breathing. The only marked difference between the male and female response was that the women reacted much more strongly if they also believed that they were in love with the man. In the case of the male subjects, their automatic motor system responded equally, whether they were in love or not. This is another reinforcement of the fact that women are strongly directed by their romantic feelings.

The erotic kiss differs from the kind of kissing that takes place between mother and child or platonic friends. Deep sexual kissing plays an indispensable role in stimulation of sexual excitement. Its importance lies in the fact that the lips, the mouth and the tongue comprise what is known as an erogenous zone, and whenever erogenous zones are stimulated the excitation spreads to the other sexual areas.

The kissing of the area around the genitals, or the genitals themselves causes the lips of the vulva to swell, become lubricated, and open in readiness for the penetrating thrust of the penis. Without necessarily being aware of it, many women equate kissing of their mouth with their vagina being entered by the penis. The male tongue going into their mouth sets an image for the genitals to follow.

Men who have become accustomed to non-responsive women, do very little kissing of any kind. Some do not like the taste of a woman's body, and they have a problem. They are the users of the female genitals as a receptacle. Some kiss only her lips. Some kiss her lips and breasts but are repulsed by her genitalia. On the other hand, some men love the entire taste of a woman's body and women should know that there are such uninhibited men.

Women are less uptight about pleasing men. Very often women, who do not reach orgasm themselves, will perform fellatio on the male, to keep his affection, and also in some cases to avoid pregnancy. However, once a trusting relationship is established, lovers should discuss equality in lovemaking.

Outercourse is skilled, extended foreplay. The man initiates the first caress, as is customary. However, this has been the case for too long. When women reverse roles, it often helps to release her pent-up sexual feeling. The outdated custom of a woman just lying still while the male does all the preliminaries of lovemaking is a major reason for female lethargy. Her lazy libido can be awakened once she learns to touch her own body and bring herself pleasure. She should also do to her man, everything that she expects him to do for her.

Jo Women

Be freely aware of all of nature's wonders as you enjoy the results of your own touching. Notice the feel of his masculinity in contrast to your own femininity. Run your hands over his body. Don't avoid or miss a spot. Get to know every hair and pore and shape of his parts and invite him to do the same with yours. Become sensually aroused through conscious participation. A lover who consciously studies her/his mate's eccentricities and special needs, becomes indispensable and very secure because, no one else can know or do as much as the original. This is the best way to avoid roving eyes.

Why Husbands and Wives Cheat

Marriage is the most difficult and challenging of all of our social institutions. Researchers say that 75% of married men cheat and 50% of wives cheat. From my many conversations with women, I believe the figures are becoming closer every day. Cheaters say they have affairs because they no longer experience the adventure of doing something different with their mates. Instead of growing together, they grow apart because intimacy has become a "day-in, day-out" routine. Men say they cheat to prove to themselves they still have the power, because their women are slow to respond.

When women cheat, they say they want romance, better communication, and more emotional support. Many women will say:

"My husband is taking me for granted."
"He lacks imagination when we make love."
"He skips foreplay. He just wants intercourse."
"I want someone who says nice things to me."

These are common complaints. Both men and women can have what they want by being aware of the many choices available to them. True intimacy comes with familiarity, with the comfortable feeling of being close to someone you can trust. Sex can expand beyond animal instinct to a spiritual encounter of the highest kind. So, why settle for rubbing skin with a stranger? New sex can be a thrilling beginning, but why not make it the overture to a life-long love affair? A new lover cannot duplicate the love that exists in a marriage, one that is built on passion and is long-lasting. No first-time lover can know the intricacies of a husband or wife's body, their idiosyncrasies.

Importance of Showing Good feelings

A person who has mastered outercourse techniques doesn't lose their lover to another. They find out what's missing and do something to correct the problem. Even if a relationship starts sliding down hill, there are lots of ways to get it back on the track. Even the most sluggish love-affair can be revived with the right formula. We all need to become more open to constructive criticism; be more demonstrative and show the other how we feel. Every man needs to know he's desirable, just as every woman needs to know she's sexually attractive.

When the wild, unbridled sex drive of a fresh relationship cools, some couples have discovered they can replace it with something more precious. Unhurried, emotionally secure, sensual intimacy which we call outercourse, is the opposite of fast intercourse. It is a way to get to know more about each other. And the more you know, the more there is to love. It takes time to develop heart strings. People who stay together in marriage or long-term relationships, find that there are hundred of tiny threads that grow between them; threads that get interwoven in a pattern of contentment. That's what makes a good marriage last.

Marriage can be an expression of immortality. When two people decide to say "I do," they expect the love to be exclusive, and they symbolize it not only by vows but by linking their bodies together in total embrace. Their lives now center around each other, their home, children and joint friendships.

This is the foundation for the security of family life and mental health for all involved. A marriage founded in honest communication can last forever when the couple remain infused with love for each other. Deep down most people would like to be married and stay married, not only to prove they can commit on the highest level, but to glow in the warmth of romantic love. The ritual of publicly promising fidelity and a lifetime of caring has a noble ring to it. All over the world, in every culture and in every religion, the ceremony of marriage is an initiation into the world of maturity, and everybody knows it. Marriage is a rite of passage that carries with it more importance than losing one's singlehood. Its success presupposes a constant process of mutual readjustment all through life. This requires great flexibility and unselfishness.

The rewards for humans are far greater than satisfying primitive urges, like the rest of the animal world. We are creatures of conscious will and subconscious power and capable of changing our minds and our behavior. We can keep love vibrant and fresh by making use of our natural inborn intelligence.

Your best chance of living up to your abilities and getting married without future problems, is to be a leisurely lover. In outercourse you take it so slow that one may beg the other to allow orgasm. But don't give in to the rush. Set aside a complete evening or an entire night of bliss. Pick a night when you don't have to get up early the next morning. Outercourse is not just a physical activity. The greatest adventure is to include the mind and emotions in your lovemaking. It is an enriching experience for both, and increases the desire for romantic love and marriage.

The most sluggish love-affair can be rekindled with the right ingredients. Once you get cooking with your own unique recipe, you'll find the most exciting lover is the one you're with right now. Sizzling sex isn't just for newcomers. Hot love is tastier when you add spice and let it simmer for as long as the mixture needs to blend together.

Marriage has gotten a bad rap, the butt of countless jokes. "Marriage is like a bank account. You put it in. You take it out. You lose interest." Not necessarily so. You can increase interest, and the pay-off is more than money. Love and trust only come with fidelity.

A special bonus is the surprising boost in health benefits that comes with making love to the same partner. You will also live longer with less stress if you settle down and give up the hit-or-miss dangerous way of life.

Consensus among researchers, is that most men and women who become unfaithful seek the chemical rush of new-sex. When new-sex becomes old routine, they find they may have forfeited love that can never be replaced. It doesn't have to end that way. The more adventurous lovers keep the home-fires burning by changing routines. This book provides hundreds of practical tools to stir the cooling embers and fan the flame of passion to great heights.

Chapter 2

You Can Rekindle Sparks of Passion

☑ *Discover the wonder of oneness*
☑ *Quiz yourself on sexual appeal*
☑ *Qualities for the ideal mate*
☑ *What love has to do with it*

 The highest form of existence is the magic of being loved and needed by just one person. When the feeling is mutual everything else is less important. Humans don't have a problem falling in love, the problem is, we fall out too soon. We need to teach people how to stay in love with each other. Most of us live in a state of emotional deprivation, surrounded by scenes of anger and violence. We are beset with ugliness of the human spirit, tensions and anxieties. Thus, many never discover how delightful a loving relationship can be. They may live out their lives without ever knowing the healing power of a warm, loving embrace. When lovers retreat from the clamor of civilization, and take a precious break for lovemaking, they tell the world tenderness is more important than materialist striving.

The time has come in human history, to re-invent romance and courtship. Without love and romance, marriage and family could vanish from the earth. Nature's greatest device for the continuation of the species, is the wonderful division of mankind into male and female. The phenomenon of contrasting sexual organs, which have the ability to pleasure one another, is the grandeur of nature's design. However, before sensual bonding can take place, humans need to satisfy their craving for emotional interaction. Behaving in a romantic way stems from a deep well of human loneliness, a need to find "the missing half." This concept crops up in all cultural literature and is as ancient as human history.

Eros, God of Love, Still Breathes

When we see curly-headed Cupid, he symbolically reminds us that romance is still trying to survive. Unfortunately, we rarely think of Cupid except on Valentine's day and only because it is a way for many businesses to sell products. Romance is more than a heart shaped box of chocolate. It's a manifestation of our need to mate and the means by which we impart deep-felt sentiments to another person.

Romantic love is the most intense human emotion and is the inspiration for countless songs of love, poetry and art expressed all over the world. Romantic expression enriches symbiotic connection and leads to deeper trust. Women's thinking has always been embroidered with romantic filigree shutting her off from the erotic needs of her body. Women are seldom moved into sexual participation without some romantic feeling. Men have much less trouble enjoying sex for its own sake, having been trained from childhood to react on a more physical level. Yet men need to receive tender love and caring as much as women do. They probably need more, judging by the violent behavior of some men.

In the past, the sexes have been dichotomized — romance for women, lust for men. The line of demarcation is dwindling. Women are getting sexier and some men are even becoming more sensitive. In the eternal longing of one to join with the other, we see an infinite wisdom distilled from billions of years of evolution. Romantic attraction animates our moods and shapes our loftiest dreams. However, only a small percentage of people have reached out for total involvement with loving feeling.

Three Levels of Male-Female Involvement

1. The first group remains at an animal level believing sex is purely physical. They avoid emotional involvement, scoff at romance and prefer risky promiscuity. Prostitution and pornography flourish from this segment.
2. Others accept the idea that romantic emotions and body are interwoven. They pride themselves as craftsmen who use love and romance to enhance sexual performance and orgasmic frequency.
3. The enlightened, smallest group enjoy sex as an expression of love. With sensitivity and spirituality, they create a physical union which celebrates harmony with the universe. If you are ready to be elevated to this plane, the last chapter will guide you in that direction.

What is This Thing Called Love?

 How do we recognize love when we find it? Why are we excited by a particular person and repulsed by others? Some men enjoy romantic courtship, but the issue is not as important to them as it is to women. On the other hand, men tend to idealize the kind of women they fall in love with. She must look beautiful according to his pre-conceived expectations. (Thank goodness beauty is in the eyes of the beholder.) A number of men have also told me she should be well behaved in public and wild in the bedroom.

Men enjoy women's erotic teasing, (but only if she lets them win out in the end). Otherwise he feels manipulated and out of control. Reluctance to romance is based on man's fear of losing emotional control.

Romance is still the surest pathway to physical trust. Men and women are of the same species but differ radically on what takes priority in a relationship. He usually lets his hormones lead the way, while she prefers romantic trimmings. *Both genders need both.* And when they have the need fulfilled, their union will last, whether they choose to marry or just live together.

Advice to Men

If you want her to really open up to you, show emotional feelings. Romantic beginnings result in intimacy that is memorable. Without exchanging sensitive feeling, much of sex is routine and forgettable, as any sexually active person will tell you. A woman's emotional response leads the way to her physical response.

A researcher recently released results of experiments that involved the body's chemical reaction to romantic lovemaking. It showed that both men and women react with increased blood pressure, heightened circulation, quickening of pulse, and deeper breathing. The only marked difference between the male and female was that the women reacted much stronger if they also believed that they were in love with the man, and even more so, if the love was mutual. Biology reveals that the energy of love's rhythms serves to keep all of the body's numerous organs and parts working harmoniously together. When we direct our love energy outwardly, we continually refresh and strengthen ourselves as well as our partner. Sexual love is a regenerating force.

Romantic Love Happens in Two Stages

1. The first flush of infatuation. Chemical attraction starts the physical flow of adrenalin and romantic feeling adds the tingle of hormones and the titillation of oxytocin to the blood stream.

2. Familiarity leads to the comfort stage. Affection blends into attachment. You mellow out. At this level the brain secretes endorphins, the brain's natural morphine which brings a sense of 'forever-together' bliss. Illuminated by love and anchored by mutual trust, two people grow into a couple, secure in their intimacy, nurtured by sharing. Let's examine what most people say they look for in a love-partner. Here are the results from "The American Consensus Report," a poll asking: What makes the ideal mate?

1. Romancing and Loving 59%
2. Fun and Sense of Humor 57%
3. Intelligence, Good-Sense 44%
4. Honesty and Openess 37%
5. Common Interests 34%
6. Physical Good Looks 25%
7. Sexual Appeal 14%
8. Wealth, Social Status 10%

The participants in this survey were told to select more than one quality and use a scale from 1% to 100% to judge the importance of each quality. What this report clearly indicates is a vast change in attitudes.

Advice to Women

Subconsciously, women have been led to believe that there must be romantic love before their bodies are permitted, morally, to function. Very often this belief makes her overly needy. She may expect more from her man than he can give. She may ask for constant reassurance. "Tell me that you love me," is a request that shows lack of self-esteem. Men prefer more self-assurance in women. Playing hard to get can strengthen the male drive, spur his masculine gonads. His glands need to be challenged. What comes too easy loses its power to excite the libido.

This is also true about the way women judge men. If a man is overly romantic when he first meets a woman, she may think he's a "whimp" or a "dork." Nobody respects a pushover, even if he/she is sincere. A couple of decades ago, people believed that "men act romantic to get sex and women act sexy to get romance." However, attitudes are changing. Both men and women share a great need to give and accept loving, romantic feelings. Without it, people can become physically ill and emotionally unbalanced. Prisons and hospitals are filled with unloved people who were never taught the power of love.

Romantic emotions set off imagery in the right brain, which triggers the nervous system and leads to sexual arousal. While all phases of love are essential for growth and self-esteem, the most glorious of all loves is "the romantic love that brings with it the deepest kind of mature commitment." This results from identifying the lover as one's missing half, without which there is a sense of incompleteness, loneliness and despair. There is no doubt that true love is glorious and spiritually uplifting, in addition to gratifying the body and emotions.

According to a recent survey conducted by the Roper Organization, love and romance appear to be eternal. Both men and women still yearn for "true-love with a one-and-only." More than 90% felt that feelings improve in marriage and that infatuation grows into deeper emotions. About 50% expressed opinions that the trend toward equal rights for women has diminished the male sex drive. The same number believed it would be wise if women would be more sexually active in marriage without being too aggressive. When asked to explain the seeming contradiction, one young husband explained, "I want my wife to get hot easily but not to start bossing me around during sex. I still want to keep control. I don't like women to dominate me." There are some men who pay to be sexually dominated by women, but they are in the very tiny minority.

I was surprised to learn after interviewing hundreds of men that most men really do prefer just one woman, "if she's just right." This has been confirmed by a recent U.S. Sex Survey. In fact, 75% of men say it is important to have a monogamous relationship. Of course, he expects his spouse to be very special and fit into his mental diagram or lovescript.

Because the vows of marriage are looked upon as serious affirmations not only by family, religions and society, but by the couples themselves, it comes as a shock when the original attraction doesn't last. Instead of working out the lack of excitement, married people tend to seek a new partner. While there are numerous reasons people give for cheating on their mates, enough surveys have been taken to determine that sheer boredom is one of the most common factors.

Using outercourse before intercourse, people can fall back in love even if the embers seem to be cool. You can fan the flames of desire at any age and at any stage of your life by adding the romantic factor. Buying a little gift. Holding hands. A kiss on the cheek when least expected. Phoning just to say "I love you." It is never too late to show romantic love or to be loved by encouraging romantic feeling.

I once hosted a television show where I asked viewers to write to me and describe their feelings about love. Here are the best of the answers:

"True love expects nothing in return."

"Love is a combination of two people's needs and the willingness to help the other get what they want."

"I love my mate not only for what he is, but for what I am when I am with him."

"Love is a feast to celebrate with all your senses!"

"Love is involuntary, while sex is voluntary."

"Love is the desire of one person to create for another, conditions under which the person can achieve his/her highest potential."

"Love is a reservoir, if you go into a new relationship with it empty, it takes time to fill it up."

"Love is laughing at your mate's stupid jokes even if they're not funny."

"Love is always there, hiding somewhere, it's up to each of us to find it."

"Love is when two souls in solitude, greet each other with a smile."

"Love seeks to make another happy, rather than be selfishly happy."

"Someone will always love you, if you show them you love yourself."

"When love meets sexual skill, you can create a masterpiece together."

"Love is not just looking at each other, but in looking together toward the same destination."

"Respect is the shield that keeps love from breaking apart."
"Who you love, reflects to the world, who you are."
"If you want to be loved, be a lovable person."
"Without love, you can live in a palace and still feel homeless."

You Deserve Love When You Earn It

 Whether you agree with all of the above or none of the above, one truth is for sure: adults cannot expect unconditional love. This we can only receive in infancy. When we are grown we have to earn love by sending out the romantic signals that attract love. It's worth the effort because love can bring light to the darkest corners of troubled memory. With romantic affection, lovers can be each other's healers and spiritual soulmates.

The Importance of Being Loved

The natural selective instinct for family security is inherent in all living things. This attitude is highly developed in humans, due to our emotion-packed thinking. We are a tribal species, and need the assurance of family. A person may say, "I don't want any strings attached to sexual intercourse." However, even the toughest of men needs affirmations of love and tender affection. Women admit to this need more than men, because they have been accustomed to more demonstrative expressions throughout their childhoods.

Without intimate love, human life would perish from the earth. Beyond the basic sexual chemistry which leads to procreation, humans have the need for emotional bonding to ensure a life that is meaningful. Studies have shown that when infants are deprived of loving affection, they do not grow normally. Some actually wither away, no matter how well they are fed. Tender emotion felt when we are young, helps us flourish and blossom into lovable adults. When we reach adulthood, we are then able to show our lovability through romantic courtship.

Subconscious Scripts About Love

Dr. John Money, pioneer sex researcher, describes
this predestination as our "lovemaps." He tells us
that normal lovemaps develop when a healthy
pair-bonding develops, between mother and child,
at birth. This is the foundation for future sexual
health, without which romantic love is difficult.
When a physically mature person has not had
unconditional love in infancy, he/she has a tendency to behave like
a needy child in adulthood. That's where a great deal of human
suffering comes from. When we become attached to a "significant
other," chances are the significance goes deeper than merely sexual
chemistry or surface attraction. It is significant in a psychological
sense, and reaches into the subconscious warehouse of memories,
some good, and some troublesome.

The romantic love ideal eludes most people because they have
unrealistic expectations of what they require from others. Too often,
they try to use the other person to fill in some missing part of their
own emotional-sexual development. If this applies to you,
remember, you can always get someone to love you—even if you
have to do it yourself! And when you love yourself, the rest comes
easy.

Fill in the Missing Pieces

So how can you tell if it's the "real" thing or just a flash in the pan?
Depending on what you're searching for, you try to fill in the
missing pieces of your own personal "jigsaw puzzle." Some people
who missed friendships during their childhood years, need that
missing piece. For them, you must try to fill the space of being a
good childlike friend and share playfulness. Others passed through
a difficult adolescence. They need to make up for the times they
missed, the social fun, the flirting and the sharing of sexual
information. Having missed the exploration, they find a barrier
exists that prevents them from experiencing what they missed.

When a love-mate fits your puzzle space, it brings a sense of completion—the pot of gold at the end of the rainbow.

The few lucky ones, who come from well functioning families, usually grow up into full maturity with some inbred sexual confidence. For them, love is a romantic adventure, with courtship a high priority. They know how to relate because they have seen it happen. They know that love lasts longer and feels stronger, when it has a romantic beginning. Unfortunately, most young people have a limited idea of what romance is. They learn more, both good and bad, from television than they do at home.

A common misconception confines romance merely to the rites of courtship—poetic words, the long-stemmed rose—but there is something deeper than conventional niceties. The most romantic thing anyone can do is soothe the other's pain from childhood. Two people, who sincerely care about each other, listen to each other, and ask questions to understand where the other person is coming from. Good lovers can fill the gaps from childhood neglect, nurturing each other's needs and building mutual self-esteem. Real love follows the romantic overture. It can only flower fully when one mate gets to know the other for who they really are, not who they imagine the person to be. Knowing that person as a human being with frailties, adds to the loving feeling.

Familiar qualities in another person gives us a sense of comfort and the ability to get closer. Looks figure into the equation as well. A person does not need to be beautiful or handsome but rather to fit the preconceived image cultivated within his or her family. A woman can be short or chubby and some man will think she is perfect. A man might be skinny and balding and stir the passion of a woman who loved her father with similar looks. It isn't always the appearance. The chemical stimulation can be triggered by a glance, a certain walk or attitude. We feel attracted to people who stir our distant memories of intimacy and trust. All of these factors form the diagram which molds our behavior toward the opposite sex. Sometimes the map or script needs altering before two people can become compatible.

The basic truth is: We have to learn what makes the other sex tick, before we can expect real love to click. The next step involves discovering each other's hidden qualities. The greatest adventure in life is to explore the mind and emotions of your lover, especially as you curl up in each other's arms. It is an enriching experience for both, as they peel away "the layers of the onion" and get to the core of who they really are. From this, shared values develop, which cement the foundation of fidelity. Love is not an external manifestation of life but the real stuff out of which a worthwhile life is fashioned.

When Lovers Become Strangers

Why does break-up cause such devastating heartbreak? Why does it so often turn out to crush the human spirit? Where did the love go? People wonder and worry. The scenario follows a familiar pattern: She loves him. He loves her. They are so attracted they are able to obliterate the need for all others. They feel complete, ecstatic in each other's arms. They both feel sure this will be a long-term success. Then one of them falls out of love and neither of them understands why.

Is long-lasting love too much to expect? Why do some relationships flourish while others flounder? Fortunately, there are some answers. Yes, you can enjoy long lasting love. You can make it happen. To begin with, you must be aware of your early programming and the limitation it placed upon you. Also, investigate the background of your mate. Only then can you understand just what each of you can expect from the other, and whether you both are making the right choice in a partner.

Choosing the right mate should not be based on superficial similarities, nor the popular misconception about the attraction of opposites. Opposites eventually clash. When a couple have cultural similarities of family and moral values, they not only tend to remain together but have less conflicts in the relationship.

The image of one true love is conditioned in the subconscious mind, from early childhood. Each person enters adulthood with his or her own unique blueprint (like an architect's diagram) for falling in love with another person. Often, it is based on feelings for our parent of the opposite gender.

Sticking to the same mate optimizes a man's sexual potential and allows his full sensuality to flourish. Knowing how and where to touch his particular woman, the varieties of pleasuring her, what she likes him to say and when to say it, sets up bridges of communication. This leads to long-term fidelity which is the highest path to marital unity. Harmony of mind, body and soul leads to a lasting union because two lovers become one couple.Blended together, one half doesn't know where he lets off and she begins.

Women have a biological need to attract the opposite sex. The average woman spends vasts amounts of money and time to get her man. It's estimated that most women devote four hours of each day to a combination of shopping, grooming and planning their conquests. This includes time spent on diet products, special body-shaping exercises and a host of skin products for every inch of her body. The amount of money can only be estimated, but the figures are sure to be astronomical.

And then what happens when she finally attracts her man? The sad fact is that once having attracted a mate she often does not know what to do with him. Her family has encouraged her motivation to attract sexual attention for marriage, but she is ill-prepared to help the relationship grow into a long-lasting, meaningful one that leads to marriage. The best of men have been confused by this duality— first she attracts and then she rejects him.

They've been taught to believe that there must be romantic love before their bodies are permitted to function. He can't do it for her. Even the best of lovers can only help, if she is emotionally ready and physically willing. To bridge the gap between her present state of resistance and full maturity, she must assume the major responsibility for her sexuality - right now. Only assertive action on her part, can successfully eradicate the repressive habits retained from her past.

One wonders why so few women make a concerted attempt to do something about their sexual lack of development. The truth is that most are not even aware of having a problem. They think the way they are is normal. They assume that the condition of their genitals and style of performance is about the same as everyone else's. They often rationalize that all women are just less capable than their masculine counterparts.

Because it is so difficult for men to live up to their macho image, a woman in love should nurture and build her man's ability. While sexual intercourse is often automatic with men, love-making is not automatically part of their lovestyle. The emotional side of love-making has been played down among men as a sign of weakness. Yet, if women can help them become more expressive emotionally, men can add many healthy years to their lives.

Men who are sensitive and freely express loving feelings usually were nurtured early in life. Mother-lovers make good women-lovers. They trust flesh-to-flesh contact with the female. Men who have not received sufficient hugging and kissing in early life, are less able to show feelings, and therefore require more understanding and re-training. Such men carry with them fear of rejection and have a short fuse where female criticism is concerned. They want love but they haven't learned to trust it.

There are Five Kinds of Love

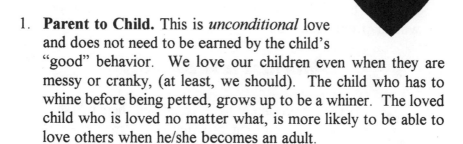

We need all kinds to give us the self-esteem necessary for emotional and sexual health in adulthood.

1. **Parent to Child.** This is *unconditional* love and does not need to be earned by the child's "good" behavior. We love our children even when they are messy or cranky, (at least, we should). The child who has to whine before being petted, grows up to be a whiner. The loved child who is loved no matter what, is more likely to be able to love others when he/she becomes an adult.

2. **Love for Family.** We are lucky if we grow up in a family where parents and siblings show love for one another. When children witness parents fighting, they feel anxiety and begin to believe marriages do not work. People from dysfunctional families seldom have long-lasting marriages themselves, because they do not know how to communicate without anger.

3. **Love for Friends.** This is a continuation of loving that extends out of childhood experiences within the family. Where there has been insufficient affection shown to a child, the young person will demonstrate this lack by having problems making friends. She or he may try too hard to be liked, and be so overly generous to others, that they retreat from the pursuer in embarrassment.

4. **Love for One's Self.** Self-esteem, a sense of worthiness is a natural outgrowth of good loving strokes from infancy to adulthood. Proper regard for one's self insures a healthy respect from others, without which one cannot truly be loved by anyone. Self-awareness puts you in charge of your life. You are able to make rational decisions, based on inner harmony, balanced with the needs of others.

5. **Romantic Love.** This provides an opportunity for the fullest expression of both physical and emotional intimacy. It includes the most passionate love, a natural outgrowth of self-love and the ability to trust another. At its best, the primitive psyche gives up the isolation of self, and unites with another into a union where two think and behave for mutual fulfillment. Before this ideal can be accomplished, lovers must help heal each other's wounds from childhood.

Men Need to be Babied

Men are more likely to have missed their full share of babying through their growing years, from the time of birth until adulthood. It has been researched and proven that male babies receive less physical handling, holding and cuddling than female infants do. One of the gender myths is that showing too much attention to a male baby will somehow make him less manly.

From the moment a male child emerges from the womb, he receives less demonstrative affection. Because males are treated in a less emotional manner, they grow up unable to show the emotions that they feel. This explains why most men have to be taught how to be romantic.

Baby girls, on the other hand, are petted and played with twice as much as their male counterparts. However, the negative dichotomy arises for females during adolescence, when they are not permitted the same degree of sexual freedom as males. Parents worry less when a teenage male goes out in the evening than they do if the child happens to be female and of the same age. Girls are warned about possible attacks, rape and molestation. They are told not to allow boyfriends to touch their intimate parts. And they are given rules about touching themselves. Most women grow up never having masturbated. The repercussions of this inhibiting training is that they find their sensory responses to be less than their male companion.

An interesting thing happens when we cohabit with a mate over a long period of time. In the caring and sharing of love with another person, we tend to take on some of their characteristics. So it's important to like the person you chose, as well as be physically attracted to him/her. We fall in love based on the early design of our lovemaps, or lovescript, but we like people based on what we learn about them from real life experience. When the two factors are in opposition, there's trouble in paradise. A case, in point, is the woman who needs to be treated with a lot of tenderness because she missed this quality from her father. She meets a man who is especially sentimental, and she falls in love. However, as time goes by, she may see him as a weakling, and now doesn't like the very quality that attracted her in the first place. This is a sign of her growing-up. However, the growth should have happened in her childhood.

No matter how you describe it, we all want to love and be loved, and the less you've received in your childhood, the more you need right now. Needing, yet not knowing precisely what we are seeking, leads us down pathways that can become a maze. This is the cause for needy unfulfilled women choosing "father figures." Child molesters are an extreme example of arrested development. We find on closer investigation that such people are unhappily tied to the past and are subconsciously attempting to fill the gap at an inappropriate time with the wrong person. They are reversing roles in an attempt to gain power that was taken from them.

Multi-Faceted Love

Love is a complex emotion that is not easy to demystify. Sometimes we get false signals based on teenage disappointment in love. Immature love is when you love the way the other person makes you feel, though you know nothing or very little about him/her. It doesn't take into account whether or not there are shared interests. Mature love is when you love the person as he/she *really is*. That takes some time, unless the object of your affections is a simpleton. *Mature love reaches beyond passion; it includes compassion.*

Whereas passion is the wild stirring from within, compassion is the reaching out to look into the other's heart and soul and understand where he/she is coming from. Compassion means being a caring friend. "I love you for all that you have suffered and endured," is an expression of compassion. Becoming friends before lovers, leads to slow-love and gives both partners time to appraise each other for possible lifetime companions.

Whenever attraction occurs, actual chemical changes occur in the brain. This excites the flow of hormones which motivate us to move closer to the object of our affection. Mae West was right when she said, "Sex is an emotion put into motion." She didn't know why it happens, then. But we do now. There is a rush of adrenalin, which can excite the emotions to want to get closer to the source of excitement.

Many men complain that women feel too much "emotion" and resist getting into "motion." When women are not romantically involved, their senses also remain uninvolved. Except for prostitution, women seldom participate in sex unless there is an emotional connection. The desire to satisfy psychological needs is uppermost with most women, before passion is released. This is the factor associated with courtship. In this age of fast food, fast cars and fast sex, many people are not even aware of what leisurely courtship could be.

All through history, the coming together of man and woman was an event of high esteem. Connected to religious rites, man pursued woman to validate his manhood. Even in the most primitive cultures, there is a courtship period during which the male attempts to win the favor of the female. Flowers, gifts, and feats of derring-do, tell the lucky woman that his intentions are sincere. The primitive female, assured of his devotion and commitment, responds with romantic acceptance; she sings, dances and feeds him delicacies. Romance and chivalry are not only part of primitive sexuality, these noble feelings are intertwined in all of human history. The heroic deeds of men throughout the medieval period, for example, were often based on the romantic desire to win the hand of "the fair lady."

Many therapists feel that the personality changes in women since sexual liberation has caused romance and courtship to be considered obsolete. Why bother to make a conquest by doing nice things when raw sex is so pervasive?

Has Romance Disappeared?

In questioning thousands of people at lectures, television and radio, I have come to the conclusion that the era of sexual liberation made sex partners so accessible, that romance has been largely ignored. And people miss it and wish it would return. We need romantic love for mental, emotional, and physical health. Happily, it's on its way back and this book is part of the endeavor.

Even those you would least expect to settle down, are doing just that. Warren Beatty, legendary Casanova until his middle years, confessed to an interviewer: "For me, the highest level of sexual excitement is in a monogamous relationship." And I especially like what Patrick Swayze said about respecting his marriage: "I'm not interested in sex for sex sake. It has nothing to do with cheating. You're not cheating on someone else - you're cheating on yourself." Behaving in a romantic manner assures that the passion will last.

How romantic we are, depends in large measure, on how romantic our parents were. Romantic behavior is learned by example. A young man about to embark on his first act of courtship will bring his date flowers if his father behaved that way toward his mother. If he has never seen courtship he may have to learn from some other source or miss the best part of intimacy. Lovescripts form the patterns of success or failure in making the right love connection, and are the direct result of something we learn in our childhood years.

This is where the first drafts of our lovescripts are designed. Lovescripts become the underlying programming we follow throughout all of our future intimate relationships. The style in which our parents addressed each other, their tone of voice, the choice of words, all have a lasting effect on us. Did they say endearing or insulting things? Most important, what kind of touching went on between them? Were there gentle strokes or physical abuse? Whether parents had fun together in front of their children will determine how their children will behave toward their oun mates later on. Fortunately, our lovescripts can be altered with the methodology I have developed over twenty five years as a maritial therapist. One thing is sure; if we have been under-supplied with demonstrative love, we tend to be overly needy as we attempt to fill in the missing gap.

When we grow up physically and are ready for the possibility of love entering our lives, we are often still infants emotionally, with an unfulfilled desire to be loved, rather than mature enough to exchange it. When this happens, people find themselves in a gridlock, immobilized between the ties to the past and the drive to push onward toward the future.

Emotional behavior starts at the moment of birth and when an infant is denied its birthright of being wanted and cherished, the problem of deprivation can be long-lasting. We are born with only an intense need to receive love, but it's the rare person who learns to love in return. Reciprocal love is learned only by example. When people suffer rejection in childhood they tend to cling to the low end of the maturity scale. We've all met individuals who rely on someone else to fill in the gaps along the bumpy road to adulthood. This kind of inappropriate parenting can become tedious to the one who is carrying the burden. The imbalance of one mate giving more than the other, eventually causes breakups and in most cases neither party knows what went wrong. Immature people lack sufficient self-esteem to function independently. They simply did not receive a firm foundation from their families and therefore, need constant reminders that they are lovable.

"Tell me that you love me," is a common request repeated again and again, by the person who does not love himself/herself. More mature people don't do as much "leeching" because they have a solid sense of who they are. They react thoughtfully and behave reasonably, rather than impulsively and over-emotionally. They can sustain long-term love based not only on feeling but on intelligence and reasonable communication. The bottom line is that an immature person wants more love than they give and in trying too hard, ends up losing the connection to the other person who has become weary of the one-sided burden.

Before we can learn how to give love, we have to know what it is. Poets write about it, songsters sing about it; some people even die for it. Yet, it is rare that two people will agree on what it is. The problem is that every individual can only describe his own subjective version based on personal experience which is connected to earlier impressions. We want it, but don't know how to handle it once we get it. Nonetheless, we keep on trying to comprehend this elusive, ephemeral state of being.

Various descriptions include words like excitement, rapture, enchantment, intense happiness, a strong desire to please, to satisfy, to care and share—the list goes on and on. None of us are innately versed in the best way to impart messages of love to one another.

Love confuses us with its web of complex signals received from others who are probably just as bewildered, and equally in need of reinforcement as the recipient, rather than the giver. Who starts the flow of love from one person to the other? That's easy. It's always the person who has more to give. The giving person is the one with the greatest sense of confidence, an outgrowth of self-love, which grew in the fertile soil of validation during childhood. When self-love is missing, fear of rejection prevents an individual from risking a situation which may prove painful.

Can you trust the first flush of chemical attraction? Maybe "yes" and maybe "no." Psychologists disagree. Some believe that love at first sight may be the most valid kind of all, if our emotional memories are pleasant ones. Because we carry in the warehouse of our minds, impressions of what is lovable based upon our earliest treatment, we are eternally pre-disposed to select and be selected based on mental diaries recorded in our subconscious.

Love choices are based on the law of the self-fulfilling prophecy. Keep in mind, what we conceive and believe, we tend to achieve. This can also be a negative factor when a person has been pre-conditioned to expect abuse and family discord. They "conceive and believe" that the troublesome situation is normal.

The expectations of what love is becomes twisted in such cases. A woman who endured physical abuse from her husband once told me that she always felt more loved when he showed his emotions in this uncontrolled manner. She said, "Every time my father hit my mother, they ended up making love."

Passive and Passionate Romance

What is romantic love, anyhow? The popular myth is that when you find it, you'll know it. But this is not necessarily so if we don't have a notion of what love means. Truth is, most of us have let love opportunities slip by, because we have rejected people who did not fit the scripts we carry with us from our childhood.

Love can be both passive and passionate, freeing and yet, enslaving. But, no matter how frustrating — we love to be in it! Love doesn't always gallop in on a white horse like the Prince in "Sleeping Beauty." It may tiptoe in on cat paws and you never notice it's there. Knowing love when you find it may be as difficult as recognizing an old friend at a high school reunion — thirty years later, fifty pounds heavier. The state of "being in love" is fraught with a great deal of contradictory emotions, both painful and pleasurable, but always entrances and enhances our state of being.

No matter how tough we are, without love, there is an aching void which gnaws at the soul. Sad to say, most people live out their entire lives without ever being able to say they experienced true love. A law of nature says "Where there is a void, that void will demand to be filled." Without love, people try to fill the void within themselves with harmful substances, trying to compensate for the emptiness they feel. Drugs, alcohol, overeating are all manifestations of the unfulfilled need that people suffer from, because they lack emotional gratification in their lives.

Added to the dependency habits are numerous ailments directly connected to lack of harmony in our emotional balance with nature. As a result, bodily health is endangered, careers destroyed, marriages ruined and children abused and abandoned. Few people know that twice as many men compared to women, break down when a close relationship goes on the rocks. For good health, everybody needs body closeness, not only for emotional security, but also for the lubrication of the body's machinery. Sexual fulfillment serves the same purpose for male and female. It refreshes, it revitalizes, and it rejuvenates every cell of the body. It also clears the mind and brings a surge of energy to every part of the anatomy. Scientists tell us that sexual love is healthy because it stimulates healthy substances which flood the circulation and nervous system. It also strengthens the immune system. Sex is stress-reducing, but when love is added, you get that indescribable inner contentment that goes beyond the physical.

Behavior scientists tell us that love shapes the course of individual lives, families, countries and even world affairs. No matter how famous or rich people may be, they are still subject to this fundamental need to take part in the continuity of life.

Don't Allow Yourself to be Victimized

Some people attract the opposite of love. They are the victims of aggressive, hostile people, and don't know how to change their situation. Many women choose men who emulate the brutal behavior of their last mate or their fathers. Still, they weep on television talk shows, insisting they want someone to make them happy. Happiness cannot be applied like a tatoo. It is an inside job. Nothing can happen until you are aware and believe you are worthy of being loved. Tell yourself, "I have earned love and deserve it!"

Enjoying sex is the affirmation of "making love to oneself." It's a way of asserting one's worthiness and lovability. The aware person is inner-directed and self-protected against the intrusion of maliciousness.

Admitting that the degree of neediness differs in various people, there are several basic truths about love that we all share. We all want to be loved even if we behave in a less than lovable way. There's a pervasive desire to re-create an adult version of the warm, intimate qualities which are characteristic of infancy, qualities we should have experienced in the relationship between mother and child. Reciprocal emotion between infant and mother is one of tender nurturing, because the mother is the primary giver of life. The person who has missed the flesh-bonding with the mother, needs an abundance of reassurance of being loved.

Today's father is expected to also show his love by sharing in the every day caring of the child. In addition, he is expected to be the main provider of nourishment to sustain the life of the child. Also, he has traditionally been viewed as a necessary role-model to help a child develop confidence and courage and other so-called "masculine traits." While this appears to be an ideal situation, it hasn't always proved practical. It has been said that some women have become the men they couldn't find in their lives. They aclimate to being the main provider in the one-parent homes. Fully one-half of the families raising children are doing so in one-parent homes.

While a two-parent upbringing is known to be the most beneficial in raising a well-balanced child, many children are forced to manage with just one parent. Lasting marriage is preferable, because it provides more emotional security and the foundation for confident living and loving.

Love's magic is believing it will last forever. When it doesn't, mental and physcial health are affected. A research chemist released the results of experiments that involved the body's chemical reaction to falling in love. In addition to the assortment of hormones and adrenaline, the study showed that both men and women react with increased blood pressure, heightened circulation, quickening of pulse, and deeper breathing. The only marked difference between the male and female responses was that the women reacted much more strongly if the man also behaved as if marriage might happen, or at least possibilities of prolonged commitment.

Love should be part of every facet of our every day lives. Unfortunately, we are more aware of hatred than loving. Human beings are motivated by two basic drives. One is the force of love and the other hatred or aggression. The interaction of these instincts propels our emotional behavior. We need to find a way all over the world for people to love and be loved. This is the immortal flow of energy that nourishes us and dissolves the hostility brought to our attention every time we turn on television or open a newspaper. When love and knowledge get together we can create a masterpiece. Instead of gazing with suspicion at each other, we begin looking together in the same direction, toward a happier destination. This is not only true of individuals, but of races and nations, as well.

Chapter 3

Lovers are Made not Born

☑ *Five kinds of love we all need*
☑ *Male and female sexual anatomy*
☑ *Sexuality and substance abuse*
☑ *The power of sexual mind-control*

 Eighty percent of American couples experience sexual difficulties at some point in their relationships; and it's not his fault or her fault. In most cases it's because a dull routine sets in. Boredom is easily overcome because there is no area of human behavior with as many possible variations as sexual performance. Experimentation in sex is a universal pastime. Anyone can learn to be a great lover, if she/he wants to. Since the beginning of time, lovers have experimented with turn-ons such as aphrodisiacs, erotic music and at least 1,000 variations in sexual positions. But it is only in the last decade that the *connection between sex and the mind* has become apparent.

When the bedroom, becomes the boredroom, many married people have affairs trying to regain the spark of youthful passion. They believe they need variety to spice-up sex. Sure they do. Variety is great. But that doesn't mean it has to be with a different partner. Keep the one you've got and use your mind to add variety to your lovemaking behavior. You have the power to employ all the lovemaking secrets of the ages, if you keep an open mind. Your greatest sexual performance is between your ears, not your thighs. Your genitals merely react to the triggers set off in your brain. The best news yet, is that everyone with a modicum of intelligence can control the responses of their sex organs to sensory stimulation.

Men, more than women are trapped in a tantalizing fantasy that having scores of sex partners adds to their manhood. The opposite is true. Really satisfying one woman takes a real man who knows what he is doing. Fidelity doesn't rob you of sexual freedom. On the contrary, it brings peace of mind, which is the deeper freedom and allows you to do things you wouldn't do with a stranger. Comedian Robin Williams expressed this very well when he said: "Am I going to run around now? No, I am at peace with myself. It's something like, 'God, I don't want to blow this. This is wonderful stuff.'"

Intimacy begins with communication. Lovers have to adapt to each other's ideas and habits. They enter the relationship with individual programs. When they edit their two lovescripts into one, both lovers agree on a way of life that is comfortable for both. They need to accept the fact that lovers often have different needs in a relationship. We are not always aware of this and have to be flexible so that we can eventually fulfill each other's desires.

Superior lovemanship is a learned skill. Nobody is born a great lover, but anyone can become one, if they really want to. Knowledge and motivation are the trusty tools which rebuild patterns of thinking. It is the self-directed thought which changes behavior. Knowledge can remodel our sexual responses the way we really wish them to be. First of all, it takes mutual trust, which develops out of honest communication.

Share Your Secret Desires

Based on our personal mysteries, we tend to avoid communication and keep our deep secrets to ourselves. Instead of talking things out, we rewrite mates according to the part we need them to play in our script of life. People are not puppets and come to resent having their strings manipulated. People who communicate become their own string-puller, and fulfill their own life story. Each of us exists inside the boundaries of shared communication and we resist having our space violated. We all require, whether child or adult, the autonomy of self-realization. A spouse should help us achieve that status without resentment. Men, especially, have to not only allow, but also assist women to fulfill their deepest desires.

To women. Become aware of all of nature's wonders as you enjoy the results of your own sensuality. Reach out and feel his masculinity in contrast to your own femininity. Let your hands wander. Explore his body just for the fun of it. Run your hands over his buttocks. Don't avoid or miss a spot. Get to know every hair and pore of his body and invite him to do the same with yours. Become sensually aroused by describing each part as you touch it.

If your partner is one who becomes overstimulated too quickly, it is sometimes best to direct your needs toward your own arousal at the beginning. Give him instructions. When you both join in practicing, the man becomes adept at his own control. Don't be prudish about telling him what you want him to do. We only get in life what we ask for, and it is no longer chic to be used by a man as a receptacle in one-sided selfish sex.

The greatest adventure in life is when two lovers explore each other's minds and emotions. It is an enriching experience for both as they peel away "the outer layers of the onion" and get to the core. From this process, shared feelings develop, which cement the foundation of future fidelity.

The best way to communicate is a direct question. If you want to know how to pleasure your mate, why not ask? "What can I do to please you?" brings magical results. While this is true of both sexes, women especially need to be urged because the problem of shyness is more prevalent among women than men. However, a woman's level of response is not entirely her mate's responsibility. He can help or hinder her evolution to sexual maturity. Tell your lover what you enjoy and how you want him to stimulate you. Sound off! Talk it out! Whisper into his ear your secret hidden desires and see what happens. The human ear is an amazing mechanism and because of its proximity to the brain carries its message to our motor reactors quickly and forcefully.

Making Love Without Hang-ups

 No place is out of bounds. Clean, healthy bodies are entirely lovable and kissable. Not all men are comfortable about licking or touching a woman all over. Some men do very little sensuous stimultion of the female. They are users, not lovers. They are the ones who struggle to insert the penis as soon as possible and then dash away to avoid any meaningful intimacy with a woman. Women praise men who enjoy oral lovemaking.

"What a great kisser!" A newlywed female client was describing her spouse. She wasn't referring to the look of his face, but to his facility in arousing her with his mouth. The most erotc part of the body, next to the sex organs, is the mouth. Lips and tongue are not only highly sensitive to touch and taste, but perform as emotional conductors from the mind's desires.

A skilled male lover who knows what he's doing, realizes how and where to stimulate. Kissing near the genitals, causes the lips of the vulva to swell, become lubricated, and open in readiness for the penetrating thrust of the penis. Without necessarily being aware of it, many women equate kissing of their mouth with their vagina being entered by the penis.

Communicate Between the Sheets

The sexiest thing you can say when you're in bed with a lover is: *"I will do whatever you ask. I want to please you."* During petting or preliminaries, whisper this into her ear and if she is normal she will show signs of becoming aroused. Besides the ears, she will be excited by the warmth of your breath on her throat as well as her inner thighs.

For some, the palm of the hand is exciting. Licking the palm and the fingers is high on the list of stimulators. Kissing or toying with the toes is a favorite activity for some women. They prefer being the receiver of this attention.

Female Sexual Anatomy

Before a man ventures to touch a woman, he should be knowledgeable about her body — how her sexual parts function. He should learn the female erogenous zones and how to stimulate her to her maximum pleasure. Every man should know the right anatomical names for the parts of a woman's body. And a woman should know the same about her man. You will gain respect from your lover because women are tired of being referred to in one-dimensional terms. Become familiar with the vocabulary of a woman's body.

The Female Breast. A message to men: Don't pinch or squeeze. Ask her how she likes her nipples stimulated and her breasts touched. There are women whose nipples are so sensitive that they can reach orgasm when their nipples are merely caressed. Many others need simultaneous breast stimulations during the height of climatic sensation to be completely fulfilled. Once the breasts are soothed and aroused, you are now ready to make love to the rest of her erotic body.

The Pubic Area. This refers to the outside frontal part of the genitalia that is visible when a woman is in the nude. This area is also called "the Mons" and is soft and cushiony. The hair which covers this part of the genitalia may be sparse or full and of various color and may not necessarily match the hair on a woman's head.

The Clitoris. Most men are familiar with this bit of tissue. The clitoris is infinitely important as a trigger in arousal and as a means toward heightening orgasmic feeling. Once a woman is aroused sufficiently, she should not be limited to the clitoris for orgasm to take place. Any woman can train herself to be responsive to penile vaginal friction during intercourse. She can help herself by diffusing sensate focus from the clitoris to the opening of the vagina, which is the gateway to internal pleasurable feeling.

The Outer and Inner Labia. The labia are often referred to as "the lips" of the sexual organ. Actually there are two sets. The outer labia extends from the pubic area and is courser in texture than the inner labia. The inner labia extend from the clitoral hood. This tissue is highly sensitive when stroked and helps in the transition from clitoral to vaginal excitation and orgasmic centering.

The Vaginal Opening. The first third of the entrance to the vagina is generously endowed with nerve endings. The woman who has a considerate lover who takes his time will be able to combine the intense clitoral feeling with sensation on the inside of the vagina. This is important because the clitoris tends to withdraw into its "hood" at the time of orgasm. Involving the vagina in the orgasm phase of intercourse, ensures that a stronger orgasm will take place for the woman. In addition, it gives the man a sense of pride in being able to use his penis to pleasure a totally responsive woman without either of them straining to force an external orgasm. It requires that a man use control to take a little extra time before penetration.

The Controversial "G-Spot." This is named after Dr. Grafenberg, who discovered its existence. Women, when fully turned on, report they can locate a tiny area about the size of an almond on the anterior (front) wall of the vagina, behind the clitoris. This spot tends to swell during strong friction and brings orgasmic focus from the outside clitoris to the inside of the vaginal shaft. It doesn't happen every time for every sexually active woman. Unless her male lover is able to maintain an erection after penetration, she may remain locked into clitoral sensation exclusively for the rest of her life, which, for some women, seems to be sufficient.

However, she should know she has this capability, because a complete orgasm creates an automatic series of rapid spasms inside the vagina and acts as a tonic for the entire nervous system. This glandular bit of tissue has been called the vestigial prostate, just as the clitoris is referred to as the vestigial penis. In some highly aroused women, a liquid is secreted from the "G" spot, similar to male ejaculate, but without the sperm.

Men Have Hot Spots, Too

There is a male equivalent to the woman's "G-spot." In fact men have two hot spots. One is a nerve at the back of the penis, where the glans (head) is divided. This nerve correlates to the strong nerve in the female clitoris. There is also a super sensitive spot between the back of the testicles and the anal opening. There is a deep nerve in that area which accents the degree of orgasmic sensation. If his mate will press this spot as he is about to reach a peak of sensation, he will escalate ecstasy to its extreme.

Male Sex Muscles Strengthen Control. There are a series of fibers and ligaments that stretch from the buttocks toward the base of the pelvis. They entwine together along with blood vessels and nerve endings that peak sexual feeling. Any man can observe them in action by flexing them for a moment when he urinates. Some men are already familiar with this ability when they deliberately tense these muscles to improve staying power during sexual intercourse. Sometimes, in cases of retarded ejaculation, these muscles can be trained to open up and release the orgasm. The same muscles are developed to help the person hold back orgasm if he is a premature ejaculator.

Here's Something Women Should Know. Many women believe that when a man is unable to get an erection, he is rejecting them, or at least, showing indifference to their needs. Not having a penis, most women do not realize how one works. Even the average man doesn't understand how his penis functions. For most men, erection is a phenomenon over which they can marvel but cannot master, at will. Once they discover the mind-to-penis connection, mastery is within their reach.

Here's How Erections Happen. Assuming the situation is conducive to male arousal, mental signals cause the valves of each penile resevoir to expand, allowing blood circulation to pour into these distensible chambers. The chambers are fixed in place by connective, sponge-like tissue and as they distend, the penis erects and stiffens. Pressure detectors regulate the amount of circulation and balance the erection and degree of hardness. This state of performance arousal can be maintained by further mind transference by use of erotic imagery.

Why Most Men Enjoy Sex More Than Women

Too many women have the misconception that they are inferior in the design of their genitalia. Not so. The female sex machinery is just as well-supplied with sensory feeling as the male's. A woman is equally able to reach orgasm when she has erased her old lovescript and conditions herself to be orgasmic. It takes her partner's staying power and her motivation to improve. She must be ready to allow the transition from low sensation to high sensation. The world's greatest lover can't force her to improve. Change for the better begins with her own positive attitude.

Your Attitude Affects Your Anatomy

When you realize this, you gain awareness. This is the first step toward alterring your mind-set. The changeover process is speeded up when you enhance your self-image. Chances are, if you are not totally fulfilled, you are underestimating your own worthiness. In addition to seeing yourself as an attractive, normal person, consider the ways in which you can improve your physical self. Perhaps some exercise or better grooming would help. Once you look better, it is easier to feel better about yourself. If your body is in bad shape you can't expect your sexual machinery to be in great shape. However, not to worry, because we all have the power to dramatically change for the better, both emotionally and physically.

A strong self-image enables a person to be more outgoing and nurturing in a love relationship. A woman who has high self-esteem expects to be well-treated because she feels she deserves such treatment. I have never known a mature, self-evolved woman who has been abused or mistreated by men. She simply would not stand for it, because her self-image does not permit denigrating behavior from others. She sets an example by her own attitude toward her own body. Because she values herself, she cannot be devalued.

Advice for Men. The sexiest thing you can say to your partner is: *"I will do whatever you ask. I enjoy making you feel good."* During petting or foreplay, whisper this into her ear and if she is normal she will show signs of becoming aroused. Besides the ears, she will be excited by the warmth of your breath on her throat as well as her inner thighs. For some the palm of the hand is exciting. Licking the palm and the fingers is high on the list of stimulators. Toying with the toes is a favorite turn-on for some women. Ask how she feels about your using a vibrator on her. Always inquire. Inform before you perform.

Helping Your Woman Release Orgasm. First, encourage her to let you know how she is feeling, then guide her with positive suggestion and fantasy, toward intensifying her sensation. You will be surprised at the increase in her level of response. Much has been said about the need for altering positions during lovemaking. You can try every angle. But unless there is the meeting of the minds and emotions, changing physical positions will do little to optimize her pleasure.

However, if she is sensually in rapport with you, you can suggest the woman-on-top position. This assertive stance helps many women who do not function well in a submissive posture. Orgasm is connected to a sense of body control and many women are able to increase their sense of power by reversing positions.

Communicate After Orgasm. For women, the afterglow is very important. It should be so, for men, as well. This is the time when two people cuddle and share loving feeling that comes from having pleased each other. In this most intimate manner, they should affirm their fidelity. Too often the man will roll over and fall asleep without so much as a "fare-the-well."

Men Can't Fake Performance

Anxiety and the anticipation of performance failure elicits negative feelings like guilt, shame, and sometimes hostility toward the woman. Tests show that muscles tighten their grip on the blood vessels that pass into the genital area. A conditioned pattern blocks blood flow to the penis, until a sort of armor is built up in that area. The sphincter muscles tend to lock as circulation is cut off.

When a boy grows into manhood and discovers that he has sexual problems, you can be sure of one thing, nature did not intend it to be that way. Someone, somewhere said or did something contrary to the natural development of his sexual drive. Nature not only wants, but demands, healthy genital function for the continuation of life.

Living in the computer age tends to desexualize us because intense mental focus detracts from the physical instincts. The extreme result is the immunization against sensual pleasure. The rate of sexual dysfunction among men has doubled in the past decade. They are the ones who have become deconditioned to their own ability to control the pleasure syndrome of intercourse. The crippling of man's libido is just one of the manifestations of the world's general flight from natural function.

Unfortunately, some men forfeit their birthright to masculine virility because they do not know there is a natural solution to psychogenic impotence. They rarely seek help about sexual problems. Instead of sharing their concerns with a professional therapist, they blame it on other things—mostly women. This is the undercurrent of feeling among men who beat their women. Many men become seriously depressed along with their impotence. *Men commit suicide three times more often than women.* I have never met a suicidal person of either sex, who was fully functioning and enjoying great sex. Happy people are not motivated to kill themselves. Their problems begin much earlier than the immediate relationship.

Two Loving Gifts Children Need From Parents

1. Roots developed in healthy soil, and *2. Wings of confidence.* If you are the one out of ten who had this better-than-average upbringing, you're lucky. If you haven't and you've still managed to function well for yourself and lover, give yourself a well-deserved pat on the back. You are fortunate to have overcome the power the past has over the present. Some people do manage that difficult task. For them, the past serves as a reference, rather than a trap.

To appreciate how far you've come, it's good to take a look at where you're coming from. At puberty, a male unconsciously begins his search for individual sexual identity. Puberty is the miraculous unfolding of the most dramatic phenomenon of life itself. It is a time which changes not only the appearance and function of a boy's body, but his personality as well. In our hemisphere, puberty starts at about twelve and continues until sixteen or so. In other parts of the world, where the climate is hotter, it may start as young as eight or nine.

Along with the almost daily signs of maturing, a strong new curiosity springs up. For the budding male who has not had his questions fulfilled in a healthy way, insecurity sets in and his future sexual problems may already take root. The sexually informed young man is less likely to turn to bad habits like alcohol, drugs or other self-defeating behavior because he accepts himself as normal.

Puberty leads the way to adolescence, which is the apex of male virility. While puberty refers to the transitional stage from boyhood to manhood, adolescence is the arrival of manhood. It has its beginning at about the age of fifteen and lasts until about twenty. Teenagers are at the peak of their sexual capacity, biologically. However, society is not prepared to deal with this kind of energy and rarely takes into account the surge of hormones when judging the behavior of teens. This is a time when male identity is of extreme importance, and if it cannot be found at home, young men look outside the family and support groups develop. Hopefully this is manifested in sports activities, but where that is not made available, membership in gangs can be the next choice.

Although the sex drive is at its strongest, there are no guilt-free erections allowed to the young. An adolescent is capable of getting an erection at almost any time and with very little provocation, but this may be a cause for embarrassment rather than pride. In later years, when he becomes middle-aged, an erection will be a reason for pride instead. Perhaps this is because our world and its mores are controlled by people past middle-age. In any case it will help you to understand how the mental emotional factor has left its mark on your own sexual image.

Suppressed Sexual Energy Explodes

The rush of hormones and adrenalin that the young are forced to inhibit does not evaporate. Sometimes it becomes converted into hostile activities. When bodily pleasure is denied, the animal instinct is frustrated and wants to strike back. In spite of widely held beliefs, young men do not find sexual partners easily. Girls are concerned, and rightly so, about pregnancy and so they reject most advances. When this happens the force for loving often is converted into hatred toward women. This may not show itself in immediate overt behavior but is subconsciously stored and released later, in inappropriate situations. Most male abuse against women can be traced to early rejection by a female.

It is an acknowledged law of science that energy never disappears. It is merely transformed from one area to another. Thus, when the excess energy of the adolescent's sex drive is not released through sexual intercourse, it seeks other channels through which to throw off its excessive load of tension. The rare boy who emerges unscathed from puberty to manhood will welcome his sexuality with emphatic joy. He's comfortable with and proud of his sexual maturity. In reality, this is seldom the case, however, because just when he feels the strongest need for sex, he also gets the greatest rejection. An elderly man once told me, "When I was a teenager I had so many erections, sometimes it would embarrass me. Now when I get an erection it's a source of pride."

In every generation the spirited teenager invariably antagonizes adults, as he tries to reconcile the power of his emerging manhood with what he perceives as the absurdities of the world around him. This is a time when the young man needs the closeness of an adult that he can trust to guide him through the insecurity he is experiencing. He should be assured that anxiety about male identification is a normal occurrence with most men. One of the insecurities that bother most young men is whether they may have homosexual tendencies. If the first sexual encounter with a girl is a disappointing one, his mind may play tricks and convince him, that he is not "all man."

Widespread Fear of Homosexuality

An encounter with a homosexual or a series of experiences do not mean that a man is not "normal." Many men and women experiment or are seduced into an occasional affair with their own gender. Some seek it out to discover whether they have a preference for same-sex intercourse and then make a choice for their sexual lifestyle. A number of studies have been done which indicate that well over half of the so-called heterosexual male population has at some time indulged in same-sex intercourse. Just a short decade ago, most people regarded homosexuality as abnormal and a mental or emotional illness. The slightest identification with a homosexual was considered a permanent sexual choice. Intelligent people accept the fact that homosexuality has always existed and is here to stay.

It's important for both men and women to keep an open mind and an open door to enter into discussions on this issue. If a woman discovers that her mate had engaged in male lovemaking, she should not panic. Both men and women must realize that both genders are biologically androgynous. Neither sex is 100% male or female. We each have hormones of the opposite sex. This ensures that a male and a female will have insight where the other is concerned. There is evidence that cross-over sex is prevalent and a major cause of the spread of AIDS into the heterosexual community. Whether we are heterosexual, homosexual, or bisexual, we must all avoid the trading of body fluids, until we test negatuve and decide to stick to one partner.

What Men Should Know About Women

I asked a young woman what message she would like to give to men. Here is her answer, "I would like to tell them, first of all, that women want to have a deeper friendship before men expect them to go to bed." Today's sexually liberated woman deeply desires a new kind of relationship with her man. She looks for close rapport, the kind of interpersonal, empathetic understanding that involves her mind before her vagina. Women prize masculine vulnerability. A man should be comfortable with his emotions and not afraid to hold hands in public or to cry at a sad movie. He should be able to share his problems and listen to hers. Many men fear the assertive woman and are concerned about being controlled by such a woman. We need to examine some of the myths and platitudes which color man's opinion of women.

The modern woman is usually sexually active. She can distinguish a good lover from a user or a loser. A woman with self-esteem is not content with being treated as second best.

Too often male thinking is linked to the Victorian era belief that there are basically two kinds of women, those who are sluts and the others who are virtuous. Time for obsolete thinkers to learn this fact: *Hot women are good women not only for themselves but for their mates, as well.* Passionate women can be devoted mothers who raise their kids with a happy spirit instead of the doldrums. Tradition has flown away on winged feet. Television programs like MTV have sharply altered not only man's perception of women, but also how women see themselves.

Men Should Learn How to Kiss

Nothing tastes as sweet nor feels as soft as a lover's promising kisses. Because it involves all the senses, a kiss can bring about instant arousal. The very first kiss is a determining force for the future of the relationship. It can awaken passion, or turn a woman away, repulsed. Some of the ways that men turn women off by their kisses are:

1. **The insulting, presumptuous kiss.** This presumes a woman is ready for sex when she hasn't even made up her mind if she likes you. This is a show of selfishness because it doesn't take into consideration how the woman is feeling.
2. **The "dead-lips kiss" of non-contact.** This is the kind of kiss that seems to say, "Don't give me any of your germs." A dead kiss sends a message that the man has problems letting go his inhibitions and is squeamish about intimacy.
3. **The tense powerhouse-suction kiss.** This is performed by a man who is unable to control his animal instincts. He comes on as so eager, you get the feeling he is trying to swallow your teeth, fillings and all. Less is best, until you are both comfortable with each other.

Soul kissing should not be pushed too soon. Some people are fearful of the exchange of saliva because some medical researchers are concerned that saliva may carry some types of venereal disease.

Most women prefer the first few kisses to be affectionate, rather than extremely sexual. This kind of rapport builds trust for future sexual intercourse and lessens her restraint. A man should take his time and hold back until his woman shows readiness.

Some men avoid the touch, taste or smell of the female genitalia, while the best kind of lover accepts and loves a woman all over, inside and out. The modern, sophisticated woman knows there are all kinds and prefers the man without squeamish hang-ups. The greatest male award for being an "all-over-the-body" lover is that a woman will respond to him in the same way. Not because she is expected to, but because she wants to.

Women not only want men to take more time before sex, they also suggest that he learn as much as possible about making love. She wants him to read some books on male sexual performance, as well. He should make his woman feel very desirable and beautiful, especially if she needs the boost to her ego. Even if she is very beautiful, a woman still needs to feel that she is sexually the best mate that her lover has ever had. If he has been with many, this is even more important to her. When a man behaves in this thoughtful manner, he will be rewarded by hearing from his woman how very special he is. And he really is very special, because most men hold back compliments.

The outgoing woman wants men to know that she appreciates emotional honesty. It is no longer necessary for a real man to be emotionally tough. Macho is an obsolete, male thing. Women with self-esteem want more balance in their lover. It is a sign of strength to show deep feeling not only to the woman you love but about life in general. A man who cares about the world we live in also cherishes the person he is with. We are now seeing a glimmer of this new man emerging from the rock-hard programming of the past. Perhaps we can hope for the liberation of both sexes.

Pressure Reduces Sexual Passion

Don't push your desires too far ahead of your partner's readiness. Communicate about how you would like to make love. Give the other a chance to say yes or no. A great deal of needless tension can be eliminated if people talk honestly about their sexual feelings with each other. Encourage your mate to express herself/himself. Get to know your lover as a person before you suggest techniques that may be disagreeable. Also, be careful that you use words that turn-on, not turn-off.

Whereas men are aroused quickly by what they see, with women it's what you say and how you touch them. They usually welcome sweet-talk combined with a playful massage. This establishes relaxed ambiance and trust. Here's a little routine for men that helps communicate the idea that he is in control of his libido and there's plenty of time before sex. Dim the lights. Put on relaxing music. Use fragrant body oil and say, "This time is just for you to relax and enjoy. I expect nothing in return."

Give an Outercourse Massage

Start with the toes, rub them one by one.
Stroke the soles of both feet, leisurely.
Smooth the hands, palms and rub each finger.
Massage the arm muscles, into the shoulders.
Roll his/her body over and sit on the buttocks.
Take time to knead and manipulate the back.
Leisurely rub the insides of both thighs.
Extend the massage into the sexual organs.

Because women are slower to arouse than men, it is still standard practice for the male to "prepare the female" before penetration. Slowly stroking and kissing her erogenous zones (throat, ears, nipples, inner thighs, and so on) will send the message that she is desirable and can relax and trust you to please her.

Massage does a great deal more for a relationship than merely the relaxation it brings. Few people take enough time to touch each other all over. From birth until the last breath, everyone craves the reassurance of a tender touch. There is immeasurable therapeutic benefit from the motion of moving the muscles, which releases their grip on the nerves passing through them. There is only one thing better than receiving a massage—that's sharing a mutual massage as part of the lovemaking process. Massage between singles can be considered a delicious part of safe sex. It usually leads to shared masturbation or the use of a condom. The object is to feel good without risk.

How About "Four-Letter" Words?

Most men tend to think about sex in raunchy terms. Very few women do. It's not a question of good or bad—it's just the way it is. If a man is to get closer to a woman instead of having her withdraw, it's usually best to translate his thoughts into more acceptable words that carry romantic feeling. He should watch what he's saying until he gets to know her better. Then her own sexy vocabulary may surprise him. It actually helps a repressed woman to say "naughty words" especially if she has never said them before. Sound is a powerful force for encouraging erotic stimulation.

If the man is patient, even the most prudish woman will eventually uncover her ears and listen to the meaning of sexual words. Much of women's sexual thinking is embroidered with romanticism, fancy filigree to shield the fleshiness which she hides underneath. A caring man can lift the veil and help her to take an honest look at herself.

Once a woman is aroused, "dirty talk" may help to further stimulate her. On the other hand, if she indicates that certain words are distasteful, accommodate her reluctance for the time being. Rather than chance the problem of her being adversely affected by your choice of language, drop the crude words and replace them with romantic ones. There are many women who must be spoken to about love before they can permit themselves to be physically aroused. The man who isn't aware of this can lose his mate long before mating time.

The greatest effect on a woman's passion is the sound of her own voice! When a woman is emotionally able to admit that she is enjoying sexual pleasure, she will increase her own level of responsiveness. So, it behooves the ardent lover to persuade his mate to express her feelings during sex and afterward, as well. Acknowledging pleasure assures lovers that the next experience will be an improvement over the last one.

What Women Want Men to Know

A large percentage of women that I have interviewed, complained that their mates are "selfish lovers." In most cases they say men are too fast. And many men say women are too slow to arouse. Most women know the difference between a considerate lover and a selfish one. These days, most women have been sexually active since their teens. In spite of their participation, studies reveal that many women have been pre-conditioned to resist sexual pleasure while a large percentage of men are easily aroused. Eighty percent of couples experience sexual difficulties at some point in their relationships. Sixty percent of them break up. Too bad. They could have patched it up before it became serious.

Most men experience some power failure during prolonged foreplay and tend to rush toward penetration and completion of the act. Fortunately, most male sexual problems are psychogenic, rather than organic. Whether physical or mental, there are answers to help solve the male problem. Knowledge opens the door to change.

Here are Some Facts About Men

Five out of ten men have erectile problems periodically.
One out of five is troubled by premature ejaculation.
One out of ten suffers from retarded ejaculation.

When men are unsure about their performance they tend to behave in a self-defeating manner, even when they meet a woman who appeals to them. Many men give up sexual intercourse with women and resort to a lifetime of masturbation. Their bodies are still capable of reconditioning to make love with a partner but they "throw in the towel" and think of themselves as impotent. This is not confined to older men. I have worked with impotent men as young as twenty. Fear of failure is a downer. Few men are aware that fear, whether conscious or unconscious, is causing their dysfunction.

Some Common Male Anxieties

Fear of catching AIDS or some other sex disease.
Fear of failure to satisfy a turned-on woman.
Fear that an unwanted pregnancy will occur.
Fear of moral, legal or religious punishment.
Fear of overt or covert homosexual tendencies.
Fear of emotional commitment or getting "hooked."

Fears do not magically evaporate even when a man meets the woman he falls in love with. Unfortuantely, love does not "conquer all." In fact, for some men, meeting the right woman makes them more anxious and they become less able to function.

When fears are allowed to fester, they become self-destructive. Fears cause inverted ambivalence and the instinct for intimacy becomes clouded with apprehension. The result is overwhelming emotional stress which can seriously affect health and shorten one's lifespan. Because of this, many people build a protective shield over their emotions and avoid lovemaking altogether.

Avoid Substance Abuse

Instead of "turning-on" to the full potential of healthy eroticism, many non-functioning men and women are "spacing-out" on substances that further diminish sexual health, and threaten life itself. Drugs like tobacco, marijuana, cocaine, and alcohol eventually deaden the male sex drive. Drugs, especially marijuana, eventually will demasculinize men and defeminize women due to its chemical-effect on hormone balance.

Male Problems From Substance Abuse

1. The man who can get an erection only "some of the time."
2. The man who can get only a partial erection (semi-soft).
3. The man who tends to lose his erection inside the vagina.

4. The man who is functional only under ideal conditions.
5. The man who functions only with certain types of women.
6. The man who depends upon a fetish for his performance.

Women's Problems are Equally Appalling

1. She becomes less choosey about who she sleeps with.
2. She is a easy mark for men who use her in many ways.
3. She becomes less attentive to her grooming.
4. She tends to attract men who physically abuse her.
5. Her sex-drive diminishes with less focused sensation.
6. She becomes more susceptible to P.M.S. (pre-menstrual symdrome) and other maladies.

If you are one of the above, some of the above, or all of the above, take heart for they are all correctable. And even if you are none of the above, the reconditioning program described in this book can guide you up the ladder of your potential to become the greatest lover possible by learning complete mastery of your sex organs and their optimum function.

Things Men Should Know About Power Failure

Sexologists distinguish between primary impotence and secondary impotence. Primary impotence refers to the inability of a younger man to get an erection. Secondary impotence occurs in older men who may have functioned adequately until their later years. Masters and Johnson consider men who are performing at one quarter of their individual norm, as having secondary impotence. The younger man suffering from primary impotence is more likely to be psychologically dysfunctional but physically healthy. Young men are often inhibited and fearful, lacking sufficient sexual knowledge to give them confidence. Both primary and secondary impotence are influenced by reaction to strain, and the negative self-image it reinforces. These are the main areas of malfunction which afflict both the male and female and need to be corrected before you can become a great lover:

1. **Low Sex Drive**
   Insufficient aggressive motivation.
   Physical weakness or psychic lethargy.
   Inhibited due to a negative early experience.
2. **Erectile Problems**
   Inability to get an erection with stimulation.
   Inability to sustain an erection after insertion.
   Limitation of erection to a semi-rigid state.
3. **Ejaculatory Problem**
   Premature climax due to lack of control.
   Cannot feel sensation with ejaculation.
   Retarded ejaculation, lack of sensation.

Here are a few Others of Which Clients Have Complained

A conditioned dependency on masturbation.
Inhibition due to feelings of embarrassment.
Guilt/worry about homosexual inclinations.
Oral exclusivity with fear of penetration.
Heightened sensitivity to genital friction.
Reluctance to engage in oral stimulation.
Repugnance toward the other person's body.

All of the above problems have their origin in lack of proper training. Fortunately, what has been incorrectly learned can be unleared and better training can replace it.

Men Take Pride in Satisfying Women

Men, as well as women, need much more out of life than just sex. They really need commitment and the sense of security that family brings. They also want a woman to really love them, no matter how imperfect they may be. I was also pleasantly surprised to discover that for most men, satisfying a woman was of prime importance for his ego-gratification. It wasn't always that way, as any sexually active woman can tell you.

Men are definitely changing for the better. Ideal sexual satisfaction is no longer a man's exclusive pleasure with his woman playing the role of pleasure-giver. There is a new kind of interest on the part of the man in caring about the woman's needs. Men have graduated from just the missionary position to inviting the woman to get on top, if she wants to. Still, many men are missing the deepest fulfillment because they have difficulty showing romantic feelings. Opening up to his emotions and combining that with sexual control makes a man memorable to the lucky woman who wins such a prize for a lover.

Women Need to Get Into the Act

Women who have left the twilight zone of sexlessness, are now eagerly looking, speaking, as well as listening. They are touching, tasting, feeling and enjoying the entire aroma of sexual love. Younger women are less likely to behave like plastic people, but seem more like flesh and blood females, vibrantly alive. The most desirable kind of woman really enjoys sex with very little urging. She believes in her normalcy and is not ashamed to be horny. Many women can become this way with the patience and persistence of a good lover plus her dedication to self-training so she can become a good lover herself.

When a woman is a good lover, she can help her man sustain his sexual power. The rate of sexual dysfunction among men has doubled in the past decade and many sexologists believe this is due to the radical changes in his position of dominance. The crippling of man's libido is not because women are more liberated, but rather a result of our highly pressured way of life.

Unfortunately, some men forfeit their birthright to masculine virility because they do not know there is a natural solution to psychogenic impotence. They rarely seek help about sexual problems. Many of them become seriously depressed along with their impotence. Others become angry at women, and strike out. It may be one of the biggest secrets about the modern man, but men are not as strong emotionally as women.

Men commit suicide three times more often than women. In most cases, these men have lost their ability to function and satisfy a woman and think it is permanent. I have never met a suicidal person of either sex who was involved in a loving relationship, and enjoying great sex. Great lovers are not motivated to kill themselves, or other people. There is a solution to emotional despondency. You can release your "happy-juices" in several ways. There are four things that increase the flow of natural brain chemicals that lift our spirits. They should all be part of pre-foreplay and constitute the basis for sensual communication. This is the beginning of outercourse before intercourse.

A Few Simple Outercourse Techniques

1. Lovemaking and/or Massage
2. Relaxation and/or Meditation
3. Shared Humor and/or Laughter
4. Soft Music and/or Nude Dancing

For Men. Here's how to involve a woman's erogenous zones: Remember, women need good verbal strokes and educated petting before they trust you, relax and respond fully. Stroke her erogenous zones (throat, ears, nipples, inner thighs, and lastly, the vagina) with a little scented oil. Use finger manipulation of her clitoris, vulva and vaginal vestibule leading to the orifice, or shaft. Take her hand and encourage her to touch herself while she is stroking your penis.

Any one or all of the above, can enable both of you to achieve a state of erotic ecstasy at will.

Chapter 4

So — What is Normal?

- ☑ *Variations in size of sex organs*
- ☑ *Hangups that most men can conquer*
- ☑ *Effect of her emotions on orgasm*
- ☑ *The many ways to use a vibrator*

 If you've ever wondered, "Am I normal?," you are not alone. Most people have doubts about themselves in one way or another. If you think you are not normal, your body will not function normally. In ninety-nine out of a hundred cases, when people believe something is wrong with them, the problem is psychological rather than physical.

A person may be a famous celebrity, distinguished scientist or a world leader — she/he may be worth millions of dollars — but still feel inadequate doing a simple act that is commonplace for cats, dogs and all the animal species. The difference between human animals and the rest of the animal kingdom is our instincts have been crippled by anxiety resulting from negative pre-conditioning, concerning our normalcy based on expectations of family and society.

Worry about normalcy begins even before birth. The pregnant mother's number one concern is whether her unborn baby is normal. We really don't like being too different from the average person. Strangely enough, if you asked ten people what normal sex is, you probably would get ten different answers, because most of us grow up without ever being told this important information. Yet there are criteria with which we can gage how we compare to the norm.

Factors in Sexual Normalcy

1. Frequency of performance
2. Genital size and shape
3. Genetic predisposition
4. Attitude and behavior

In his wishful thinking, a man is always superb, but in reality, he sometimes wonders if he is even normal. Many men secretly worry if their sexual anatomy is up to the expected size, shape and performance. Men also feel inadequate when they hear stories about other men's frequency of performance. When a man has an on-going faithful relationship, he becomes more secure. Only a satisfied woman can assure a man that he is normal.

"Satisfying a woman" is considered the criterion for judging whether a man is normal or not. The judgment isn't always fair. The problem may very well rest with the woman. Many lack assurance of their physical normalcy such as weight, breast shape and size of the vagina. Women also worry about why they often have difficulty reaching orgasm. Most of us have some insecurities because we were not priviliged to develop in homes that understood normal development.

What is Normal Sexual Development?

1. **Childhood Curiosity.** From the very first day that a child notices the differences between the sexes, he/she should be told the truth in a way that is understandable. Even tiny preschoolers can comprehend the miracle of pregnancy and birth if it's explained simply.

2. **Puberty and Adolescence.** Both the school and the home play an equally important part in preparing a child for future

adulthood. The school can be a better source if parents are not knowledgeable or feel embarrassed about their own sexuality.

3. **The First Sex Experience.** If the young person is guided through the first two sex stages properly, the first intimate encounter will be a joy, filled with mutually satisfying experience. This can set the stage for a confident future with a mate.

Heading the list of concerns is how our bodies compare with others, particularly our genitalia. A close second is sexual performance. Because both the genitals and sexual activity have for decades been hidden or lied about, there is mystery and anxiety connected with both.

Both Men and Women Need Confidence

Many women think that they are not normal, because they don't reach the same peak of satisfaction their male partners do. Part of the problem is inbred in the woman herself due to restrictive training in her family. However a loving man can help her overcome this. Not all men are capable of helping women. Some are not even able to help themselves. I am encountering many couples where the problems stem from the man's lack of knowledge, rather than the woman's, as it was a decade ago.

Unfortunately, a large percentage of modern men are uncertain about whether they are as manly as they should be. He is expected to excel in everything; he must not only be a provider, husband, companion, and friend, but also a great lover. No matter how willing he may be to fulfill the expectations of society, and women, he is handicapped by lack of knowledge of how he can change for the better.

Stereotyping gender roles and behavior makes it even more difficult to be in the comfort zone of not being too far-out. Fear of being labeled feminine causes many men to submerge their natural sensitivities. They bury the soft side under a shell that often is not penetrated in an entire lifetime. In their struggle to live up to an image of macho toughness, they sometimes collapse in the attempt. Anxious anticipation of sexual failure to perform elicits negative feelings like guilt, shame, and hostility.

How Erections are Sabotaged

Tests show that when a man tries to perform under negative circumstances, the emotional pressure from within causes his muscles to tighten their grip on the blood vessels that pass into the genital area. This mind to body reflex interferes with normal function because erection can only take place when there is sufficient blood flowing into the arteries. The engorgement by the inflow of blood fluid is nature's means of maintaining rigidity.

When there is a conditioned pattern blocking impulses to the penis, a sort of resistant armor is built up in that area. As the sphincter muscles lock, the normal flow of circulation is cut off. When a boy grows into manhood and discovers that he has sexual problems, you can be sure of one thing, *nature did not intend it to be that way.* Someone, somewhere said or did something contrary to the natural development of his sexual drive. Nature not only wants, but demands, healthy genital function for the continuation of the species.

Many men have been brought up to believe that the woman is responsible for the state of his erection and whether he remains passionate over a period of time. The truth is that we are each responsible for our own sexual performance. Virility is always *inner directed and self-projected.* The part that the female plays depends on how much she cares about the man and how well the two people trust each other.

When a woman first meets a man, the first thing she hopes is that he will take time to get to know her, before he starts to push his own horny needs. This is because only a small percentage of women are able to climax solely with penis penetration. These are the women who have found lovers who are considerate and can take their time. A self-trained man can maintain rigidity after inserting his penis. However, about 40 percent of men will experience difficulty sometime, in performing adequately in a normal relationship.

No matter how serious your problem may be, do not underestimate the powerful influence that learning has upon changing behavior. Retraining can reshape and remodel your automatic reflexes, your circulation, and your mind-control over your sensation. People who become *adjusted* to a way of performing can become *de-adjusted* and learn how to reach a fulfilling level of normalcy in every way.

Stress is at the root of most male impotence. It is a symptom of our pressurized culture that just when women begin to flower sexually, men often lose their virility. Instead of rejecting such a man, a loving woman can help him regain his prowess. When men are honest they admit they need as much affection and reassurance as women do. And they should feel comfortable about asking for hugs and belly rubs when they need it.

A primary source of male insecurity is society's corporate image of what a normal man should be: A three way composite of Donald Trump, Tom Cruise and Arnold Schwarzenegger. Movies and television have hypnotized people into thinking that a truly masculine man must not only be boldly aggressive, but physically perfect. And a great money-maker, besides. Above all, as boy and as man, he is taught, that in war or in peace, in love and in business — *he must not show too much emotional feeling.*

A real man is told he must never flinch when he is in pain, nor cry when he is despondent. Outward expressions are considered *weak and feminine.* And when men lose their emotionalism, they also lose their ability to relate to women. Men will live longer and feel stronger if they allow themselves to act needy sometime. Instead of clinging to entrenched stereotypes, both genders need to adopt more of the other's gender characteristics to become fully realized and to live longer and happier lives.

Problems of sexual distress have their origin in early childhood. Parents need to show a more balanced attitude in raising children. Girls should be encouraged to behave in a more assertive manner, if a situation calls for it. Boys should be taught that it's okay to show feelings of sensitivity and reach out for affection. Sexual curiosity among both girls and boys needs to be handled in a straight-forward, unembarrassed way by parents and schools.

It's amazing how little most grown people know about their own anatomy and even less about the biology of the opposite gender. Most men describe their earliest sexual recollections as fraught with anxiety about performance before it happens and lots of guilt afterward.

Guilt and sex make antagonistic bedfellows. Tests have shown that anxiety about performance often causes premature ejaculation as well as erectile failure. Why are men so often emotionally disturbed about their sexual powerProbably because their fathers and grandfathers were. Each generation inherits the "blueprint" which shapes the house they live in — a house without doors or windows. Instead of being locked in forever, there are ways to escape.

About eighty percent of normal American couples experience sexual difficulties at some point in their relationships. It's not *his* fault or *her* fault. It's a joint problem. They probably got stuck in a rut because they didn't use their natural abilities to create action, mystery and excitement.

Without proper re-education people can remain hung-over with subconscious fear of wrong-doing even when they are engaging in a mutually shared experience during marriage. Whether it takes place in school or at home, proper sex education should provide every child with the following:

1. It should help one mature without guilt or fear.
2. Give information about how the sexual organs work.
3. Answer questions about love and sexuality.
4. Provide counsel for individual family problems.
5. It should explain masturbation is not harmful.
6. It should teach how to get along with both sexes.

 **For men who lack sexual control.** If you have not as yet developed complete self-mastery, and are inclined to become over stimulated, direct your attention away from your own body and toward arousing your partner. Keep in mind that women are usually much slower to reach orgasm than most men.   If your woman is

unusually slow and you tend to be fast, it may help you to masturbate prior to lovemaking so that you are less tense during lovemaking. Nothing is wrong if it helps bring two people closer to sexual harmony.

There are no frigid women with great lovemaking. Women who are difficult to satisfy, tell me they become concerned that the male partner will lose control after penetrating the vagina. This concern on the part of both lovers, often limits the woman's sexual satisfaction to finger manipulation. I have found in private practice with hundreds of women who have suffered this problem that when they use the sensual awareness exercises which I have described in this book, that their problem can be overcome.

Strengthen Your Sex Muscles

Sometime the problem is due to lack of physical fitness. Fortunately, flaccid sexual muscles can be easily rectified in both male and female. Once people realize they possess genital muscles, they learn to strengthen their activity. For the man this means maintaining and sustaining erection. For the woman it increases friction inside her vagina. You can exercise your sex muscles any time you choose. While driving a car. While walking. While talking. It's invisible to other people.

To Men. Your woman may need special help to release orgasm. If you encourage her to let you know how she is feeling, then guide her toward intensifying her sensation, you will be surprised at the increase in her response. Much has been said about the need for altering positions during lovemaking. But unless there is the meeting of the minds and emotions, changing physical positions will do little to optimize pleasure.

However, if she is emotionally and visually in rapport with you, suggest the woman-on-top position. This assertive stance helps many women who are used to being submissive. Orgasm is sensing one's body control. Women, as well as men, are able to increase this power.

Outercourse and Foreplay. A man does not need to keep an erection during prolonged lovemaking. As long as he gets the erection later for penetration, he is functioning in a normal manner. In various studies done on the erection, it has been determined that a man who is leisurely and unstressed can take time for foreplay and have no difficulty regaining his erection later when he needs it to satisfy his partner and himself. (In that order.)

Penetration and the Plateau. Most sexual intercourse is over quickly once a man penetrates the woman. Yet it is possible for a man to reach a level of pleasurable sensation, and then hold back climaxing. This kind of man is prized by women because she is then able to focus on her own sensations and increase her pleasure. Some men use sport images to divert themselves. One comic told me he holds back by visualizing himself as a gorilla dancing slow-motion. Others are so intent on pleasing their woman, they set their own feelings aside and talk to her about how she is feeling.

What's A Normal Orgasm?

There is a great deal more to satisfactory orgasm than skin contact. The amount of sexual pleasure depends on the degree of friction through muscle control, which exerts pressure on the nerves below the surface of the skin. When people are overly concerned about whether or not they will reach orgasm, they often strain too hard and the result is apt to restrict the sphincter muscles. These muscles are like elastic bands and when they are tensed they shut off the free flow of blood and energy. Conversely, when they are relaxed and open, circulation is increased and easily released. Orgasm is more likely to happen once the repressed person stops trying so hard and accepts the experience as a natural exchange of physical affection. My object in writing this book is to call to the reader's attention a need for us all to slow down and enhance the pleasure of the moment, rather than be goal-oriented. Climaxing is a signal that the pleasure is about over, so why rush through it, when sustaining the plateau is so meaningful?

While there are twice as many women as men who have orgasm problems, men tend to suffer more when the condition is severe and long lasting. Men with inhibited orgasm tell of pains in the groin area and prostate discomfort. For women the repression takes the form of emotional outbursts, tearfulness and a tendency to suffer with Premenstrual Syndrome(PMS). The male who is a retarded ejaculator needs the same kind of therapy that the repressed woman does. He needs to focus on feeling pleasure at the moment. Here are some hints for releasing orgasm:

1. Employ Erotic Fantasy. Imagine yourself as a person who doesn't have your problem.
2. Use Manual Manipulation. Masturbate to strong sensation before intercourse.
3. Massage While Using Vibrator. Ask your lover to massage your inner thighs while you use a vibrator.

The Roots of Female Repression

A woman's self-image of her normal functionality is formed during her most impressionable years, and sometimes is difficult to shake without psychological assistance. These deeply engraved, cerebral messages of "right" and "wrong" cause women to react negatively to stimulation. Within their mind's eye, a red light flashes "Stop" when they should get a "Go Ahead" signal. It takes many women six months to a year before they are comfortable enough to respond fully to love-making, even in the security of a marriage.

After continuous repression of instinctive sensation, the female sexual organs set up a reflex pattern of immunity, and become further desensitized to pleasurable feeling. To ensure that their daughters remain chaste until wedlock, some parents teach them to fear the consequences. Many girls are taught to mistrust and resist the advances of all males. Some are instructed that his interest in her is purely animalistic and she must avoid succumbing to her natural feelings.

Children are also unconsciously programmed by the friction between their parents. Children are never fooled by superficial attempts at covering up. When sex is lied about, children learn their lessons from this also, but not to their advantage. The fact is, all children start learning about sex from earliest infancy on, and females get the idea they are somehow less sexual than the male. This limiting conditioning is reinforced by movies, TV and media stories of abuse and mistreatment of women.

Female fear of letting go in adult love-making has its roots in the first parental "no-no" or "don't touch." This is the first page of the rule-book which can be her pattern for intimacy the rest of her life. Sexual repression starts at an early age and is directed more toward girls than boys. Parents tend to allow their sons more leeway than they do their daughters. The young woman has been trained to hold back affection to the young man. This will diminish her ability to return affection later when she wants to establish intimacy.

Repeated rejection deflates male ego and makes many young men overly aggressive to prove manliness. There are countless men of all ages who have been scarred in this manner and they carry the anger with them and sometimes explode with violence.

Basic Facts About Men's Normalcy

1. Four out of five men have erection problems periodically. It's normal.
2. One out of five is bothered by premature ejaculation, due to lack of control.
3. One out of ten has difficulty releasing orgasm and/ or ejaculating semen.

All these problems can be eliminated by using the program presented to you in the next chapter.

Women's Fears are Universal

Fear of failure is a sure way of making failure happen. Fears do not magically evaporate even when a woman meets the man she falls in love with. The most common are:

    Fear that an unwanted pregnancy will occur.

    Fear of moral, legal or religious punishment.

Fear of overt or covert homosexual tendencies.

Fear of emotional commitment or getting "hooked."

Women's fears start early and are based on watching her mother's behavior. Was her mother a person who could give, as well as receive love freely? Did she see her mother as self-confident? Was her mother comfortable with her own sexuality?

If she has modeled herself after a positive mother, she will be prepared, by good example, to look forward to sex with positive expectations, rather than with the prevalent attitude of trepidation and anxiety. The ultimate aim of loving parents is to raise a normal child capable of healthy, happy sexual function in adulthood.

Many women are disappointed in sex and conclude that they are subnormal, because they don't reach the same peak of satisfaction their male partners do. Even though reaching adulthood, they remain trapped in childhood patterns of thinking. They carry over into the sexual act an aversion to seeing themselves doing something which was once called, "not nice for a girl to do." When women cling to outmoded barriers, they lose the ability to enjoy lovemaking. One woman who violently objected to her husband's having the light on during sex explained, "I enjoy sex in the dark, but when I see my husband naked, I feel ashamed. Either the lights get turned off, or I get turned off."

Unless you are that rare woman who has never had orgasm problems, you need to do some corrective work on your responses. You will find techniques later in this book that will help you make the necessary changes. You must however, realize that your fate is in your own hands and not simply depend on how a man treats you. Women who act out their lives based on obsolete scripts, cling to adolescent sexuality, believing, "Mr. Right," will come along and wake up their dormant sexuality. Each time they are let down, they blame the man for their own inability to function, which, of course, is not his fault.

A woman can't "have her cake and eat it too." To be treated as an equal in bed and out in the world, women have to be masters of their own destinies. Equality demands responsiblity and to be a mature woman, she has to validate her body, without depending on the chance some man will put the stamp of approval on her. She is the only one that can deal with "the echoes in her mind." To put it succinctly, a person can be born with normal sexual organs (and most of us are), and still use those sexual organs in an abnormal manner.

I assure you, male or female, that you can become better than average and reach your personal maximum as a great lover. It's a matter of learning how to behave toward others and yourself. This is more important than being born average or attaining normalcy during your lifetime. Personal maximum means that you have contributed toward your own development and have re-written the original scripts from childhood. Nobody wants to be either abnormal or subnormal. We don't mind so much being average, but being below average can be disturbing.

Average is Considered the Most Normal

Breasts and penises don't have to be bigger to be normal. And you are normal even if you are less than average. First, it would help to set the criteria to understand the difference between *average* and *normal*. When we say average, numbers come to mind—"What is the mathematical result?" To get this we add a group of figures and then divide by the number of participants tested. The average American is 31 years old. The average male is 5 feet 9 1/2 inches and weighs 173 lbs. The average female is 5 feet 4 inches and weighs 140 lbs. This is according to the Census Bureau. These figures were arrived at by adding and dividing numbers.

If you want to determine if you're getting as much sex as the average American couple, check this recent U.S. sex survey: If you are between the ages of 18 to 24 years old, a rate of 12 times a month is the most common. If you are between 24-34, you should expect to be doing it about 10 times a month. If you are 35 to 45 it's 8 times and then it dwindles down to 4 times a month for couples over 45. If you are not average, don't despair. Normal covers a much wider range and most of us are normal, and a much smaller percentage are average.

Normal has a broader definition because it goes beyond numbers and includes society's expectations. To be looked upon agreeably by our peers, we must conform to the standards acceptable to the majority of the people in the type of society in which we live. Standards for judging are variable. For most people being normal means "What I do, and the way I look is normal. Therefore everyone who looks or behaves like me is normal also. Any one who doesn't is therefore, deviant or abnormal."

An example of normalcy versus deviant behavior might be a scene in a convent where a nun suddenly confronts a nudist. Under the circumstances, she is normal, and the nudist is a deviant. However, if the situation were reversed and a nun, clothed in her habit, showed up in a nudist camp, the nun would surely be the deviant. Normalcy and deviation depends on who is setting the rules and is a subjective reaction. According to social scientists, whatever body types and behaviors are most common become the considered norm. Going against the norm is always perceived as a deviation. Based on average calculations, something that doesn't upset traditional norms is socially acceptable.

Where sex is concerned, normal means: not too much or not too little; not too small or not too big; not too fast or not too slow; all boundaries form a basis for judgment by the majority setting the rules for the minority. The ideal of a one-to-one marriage with two children is normal for most people. There is something idealistic about "normalcy" because most people equate it with being perfect. It is also like a "rite of passage," as it labels you a member of the larger clan.

There has been a paucity of information about normalcy, a subject vaguely dismissed with remarks like "There is no such thing as normal." On the other hand, we are bombarded by the media with talk about abnormal behavior—teachers who molest their pupils, fathers who perpetrate sodomy upon their daughters, religious zealots who frequent houses of prostitution, bisexuals who infect their wives with AIDS, freaky fetishes, and a host of other manifestation of deviant behavior. In the area of sexual activity, it is difficult to decide what is normal. Few of us have access to the sexual secrets of other people. Even in surveys, most people do not tell the whole truth about their intimate desires and habits. We need to take the word of people who devote themselves to this kind of research. And very often their figures vary to a great extent. Human curiosity is the reason why television programs featuring sexual deviation are so popular.

Many single people avoid getting married, fearing they are not biologically normal in some way. To better understand how to judge normalcy in men and women, physical characteristics have been divided into two main classifications — Primary and Secondary.

Primary Sex Characteristics

Primary sex characteristics include all of the organs and glands which play a functional role in the work of reproduction of another life.

The Reproduction Glands

In the male. The testicles are the male reproductive glands, and produce mainly testosterone with a small amount of estrogen. The level of hormones should be tested if the male is experiencing functional problems. The prostate, a muscular organ which surrounds the urethra, at the base of the bladder, should also be checked.

In the female. Ovaries produce mainly the hormone called, estrogen. A smaller amount of androgen (a male hormone) is also excreted. If a person has a consistently low sex drive, she/he should check with a doctor to determine if the problem is glandular or stems from another source. If the disinterest is psychogenic rather than biological, meditative reconditioning can increase sexual passion dramatically. Always check out your physical organs before assuming the condition is mental.

The Normal Sexual Apparatus

In the male. The testicles, penis and prostate gland.
In the female. The uterus, vagina, labia and clitoris.

Secondary Sex Characteristics

Secondary sex characteristics are the extra-genital manifestations which differentiate the sexes, such as hair patterns, musculature, body shape, voice etc. These are also individual variables. A woman may be feminine looking yet have hair on her chest. A masculine man may have a high-pitched voice. It's the total picture that decides whether the secondary characteristics are in the normal range.

Secondary characteristics include the structure of the body. Women have narrower shoulders, whereas men have narrower hips. The posture of a male and female differ as well, and the movement of the body is either feminine or masculine due to the differences in muscular coordination. Secondary characteristics are also obvious in the texture or smoothness of the skin.

What Makes a Man Normal?

If a man is able to satisfy the woman of his choice in any way that they mutually decide, for all intents and purposes, he can consider himself normal. If he wants to reach greater heights and become a super lover, he can cultivate his techniques, timing and self control.

A normal man must be uninhibited enough to try various techniques of arousal and methods of intensifying his mate's orgasmic sensation. He must be free of squeamishness about the female body. It is considered normal for males to offer to practice cunnilingus and most women know this. Many have been accustomed to the intense sensation of oral sex and depend on it in order to reach orgasm. Although, this is expected behavior it is not a prerequisite for male normalcy. There are many other titillating things a man can do for the greatest arousal of himself and partner.

Myths About the Testicles

Many men assume that the size of the testicles influences sexual power and performance. Normal testicles do not depend upon size or shape. Most men have two testicles, with one appearing to hang lower than the other. Some men have one non-descended testicle and they are able to function perfectly well.

Any abnormality should be discussed with one's physician. A man who has extremely oversized testicles has a physical problem, usually involving his prostate and should see his doctor. However, it is an accepted fact that the sex drive is influenced mainly by thought patterns and less by the anatomical shape of any organ. Sensuality stirs the production of hormones and leads to the passion which increases blood flow and sexual energy.

What's a Normal Sized Penis?

Lanky Abraham Lincoln was once asked by a small boy how long a man's legs should be. He answered "Long enough to reach the ground." Remember, the vagina is only sensitive in the first third of its shaft, which measures about one and a half inches. So, forget everything you've been told about penis size. Really great lovers, even if undersized, can satisfy a woman better than a selfish man with a big penis.

According to sex researchers: If you measured three penises and found one was seven inches long, another six and the third four—the average size would be *five and two thirds*. The normal range includes the longest and the shortest; therefore the four inch penis is just as normal as the seven inch penis. Both can do their job equally well.

In evaluating himself, a man must take into consideration his genetic inheritance — what physical characteristics parents and grandparents handed down. Some men are so obsessed with the idea that bigger is better, that they do not feel adequate even though they are normal. Most people still carry subliminal messages from ancient times, a hangover from the days of phallic worship.

Surgical Penis Enlargements

Plastic surgeons who perform penis enlargements report a flourishing business. The results report extensions of about one to two inches. The surgery, which cost several thousand dollars, entails releasing the penile shaft from its ligaments and drawing a flap of skin from the pubic area to cover the added length. Local anesthesia is used and it takes 2 to 3 hours. They say the patient can usually resume intercourse after several weeks of healing. From reports I have heard, one should allow several months. The minor scars in the pubic area disappear as hair returns to the area. Is it worth the time, trouble, money and pain? That depends on the individual man.

In an article in Glamour Magazine, a young man who had received a 2" lengthening of his penis said he had never had a complaint from any woman he was with before the operation. On the contrary, he was self-conscious in the presence of other men. Locker room evaluations do not affect how a woman is satisfied. Only one out of ten women equate good sex with penis size. Most women want a considerate lover who takes time and behaves in a romantic way.

Lets Meet the Normal Woman

A woman's self-image of her normalcy is formed during her most impressionable years, and is difficult to shake. These deeply engraved, cerebral messages of "right" and "wrong" cause many women to react negatively to erotic stimulation. Within their mind's eye, a red light flashes "Stop" when they should get a "Go Ahead" signal.

We must all realize that our fate is in our own hands and not dependent upon how we are treated. Some women act out their lives based on obsolete gender models. They cling to an adolescent stage of sexuality, believing that "true love," embodied in "Mr. Right," will come along and wake up their dormant sexuality. That's not the way it happens, as any woman can tell you. Women who fall madly in love are disappointed when their bodies will not respond, even though their emotions are wild. A cleavage may develop between mind and body.

When a woman allows herself to think freely about sexual pleasure, she will invariably increase her sensual responses from within, rather than expect it to happen from outside her mind and body. She must allow herself to openly manifest interest in being satisfied. Her lusty thought processes will trigger her brain to send the right vibrations, to encourage orgasmic sensation. There is no way a man can force a woman to have an orgasm. Orgasm is always inner-directed and self-projected. It's her responsibility.

Once a woman decides that she, herself is responsible, that decision grants her the power to change. Improvement begins to show itself in a most dramatic way. Any woman can accomplish this and bring about remarkable changes in herself, physically, emotionally and spiritually. For most women, feelings of being loved and cherished must precede her participation in sexual intercourse. When this doesn't happen, women are usually disappointed in the physical aspect of sex.

Quantity vs One Quality Orgasm

How about female multiple orgasm? For the rare woman, several climaxes may follow closely during uninterrupted stimulation. These peak experiences are accompanied by vaginal contractions of short duration. Another kind of multiple orgasmic experience that is described as being fully satisfying, is with strong vaginal contractions and rest periods between each coital union. A woman is normal even if she does not have multiple orgasms, or go wild every time she makes love. Unrealistic thinking has doomed many women as well as men to think of themselves as sexual failures when they are in fact, in the normal range and can improve tremendously with training.

A normal woman is one who can relax during sex, secure in her mind that orgasm will take place easily if she so desires. Above all, she does not feel totally dependent upon her man's skill to make her climax, as so many women do. There are some women so resistant they can tax the virility and patience of the strongest male. When orgasm is elusive, sometimes it is because a woman is disinterested in making love with a particular person. Sometimes lack of communication is the culprit. Unconscious conflicts should be discussed until an understanding is reached.

If you can't make it, don't fake it! It is not normal to act as if you are climaxing just to make the man feel normal. Some women fake orgasm to avoid confrontation about their own normalcy. Others figure they are with a lousy lover and want to get it over with. Before blaming men, women should check out their own limitations and then proceed to eliminate the obstacles to full participation. For many years it was considered normal for women to have a lower sex drive than men. These days that notion is being challenged.

In evaluating her normalcy, a woman must ask herself if she is dependent on special stimulation. A normal, sexually mature woman should not have to rely only on a single form of stimulation, such as oral sex (cunnilingus, finger manipulation or vibrator for reaching her climax). All of these methods are fine, but should not be used exclusively. This is important so that she lets her inhibitions go and freely enjoy sensual pleasure with a lover, no matter what variations they use.

For some women, orgasm involves only the clitoris; for a lesser number, only the vagina. Still others can manage to combine both. Debating which is preferable, clitoral or vaginal, is pointless. *Women need to get it all together.* Whatever means and in whatever area it takes place, orgasm is necessary and natural for all. However, the struggle to achieve orgasm as an absolute goal should be discarded and the pure pleasure of the moment emphasized.

Women who reach orgasm with total involvement of all genital tissue, both internally and externally, are possibly getting more psychological satisfaction than women who limit themselves to clitoral orgasm. We cannot even be sure of that, for who is to judge and make the comparison?

There are women who have all three types of orgasm -clitoral, vaginal, and total involvement. One of them expressed her feelings this way, "Both are preferable to either or neither. But either is better than neither."

Whatever sensation exists, the mind has the power to increase the pleasure many times over, once we learn how to use sensate focus with imagery.

Correction of "Hooded Clitoris"

There is a rarely discussed problem that limits an unknown number of women from achieving strong sexual feeling. While we know that physical defects in genital structure are rare, there is a percentage of women, (no one knows how many), who are sexually handicapped due to a condition called "Hooded Clitoris," which limits erotic sensation because the clitoris is pulled up into the pubic area causing a limited amount of sensitive tissue to be exposed to friction and fondling.

The problem consists of adhesions which restrict the clitoris to an immobile position high in the cleft of the labia. This obstruction can easily be remedied, often in the doctor's office without going to a hospital for surgery. Where surgery is necessary, it consists of a simple procedure of snipping a bit of tissue to free the clitoris, which then descends closer to the vaginal opening. This procedure is done with a local anesthetic which relaxes the prepuce sufficiently so that it is able to retract behind the glans of the clitoris. In this way, the interfering tissue is cleared away from the nerve endings, permitting greater feeling. Women who have this condition are rarely aware of it, because doctors do not look for clitoral adhesions unless a woman calls attention to the problem.

In a study conducted by Dr. Leo Wollman, Medical Sex Therapist, of New York City, the following information is significant: The results of analyzing 100 cases of Hooded Clitoris showed that 92 women reported intensified sensation, more rapid response, and a greater number of orgasms after the operation.

Vigorous Sex Requires a Healthy Body

Great sex requires lots of energy as well as muscle control. There are over six hundred muscle complexes covering the two hundred bones in your body. These muscles contract and relax constantly, even when you sleep. Unresolved emotional and mental tension causes them to tighten unconsciously. When this occurs, muscles exert pressure on the nerves that pass through them. Residual tension very often settles into the pelvic area and interference is set up.

The slowing down of circulation to the penis, for example, causes difficulty in achieving erection and maintaining rigidity. For women, this lack of erotic circulation manifests itself in lowered sex drive and the retardation of orgasm. Accumulated muscle tension has long been recognized by the medical profession not only as a source of sexual malfunction, but as one of the causes of a vast number of psychosomatic ailments as well.

Your body is a marvelous example of engineering excellence. It is an engine built to power every organ it contains. But energy that is dissipated is like steam escaping from faulty valves. If you waste steam, you have that much less to activate your pistons. Keep in mind that the human body does not come with spare parts so take care of the ones you've got. They haven't perfected sex organ *transplants* yet, although they are doing big business with implants for the penis that refuses to erect. Many of the painful implant operations could be avoided with the corrective exercises in this book.

Can anyone improve? Yes. Almost everyone is susceptible to the process of change. The sex drive is an energy switch that can be reversed from negative to positive. Most dysfunction is based on *bad sex habits*, rather than biological imbalance. Good sex habits can strengthen the ties between two people and draw them very close.

Some love troubles are based on personality clashes, fear of the opposite sex, wrong training in the family you came from and a host of other handicaps that people carry into new relationships. Because subconscious thought and sexual performance are closely linked, a reconditioning program can eliminate the problems and lead you to the sunny side of the street.

Sexual health is more than erections and orgasms. To function on an optimum level we need to know how to keep our bodies vigorous and also relaxed. An active sex life burns up a great deal of energy, so a properly balanced diet is essential. If you don't know what you should eat, find out. Go to a health food store and ask questions. Incorrect eating curtails biological function, for we are what we eat; make no mistake about that. A listless lover may be suffering from poor nutrition - aside from a poor emotional balance.

The amount of empty calories consumed by the average person is astronomical. Foods such as fresh vegetables, raw fruits, whole grains and fish are top foods for sexual vitality. Conversely, highly processed foods such as ice cream, cake and sweets are commercialized to excess and do little more than build fatty tissue on the human frame. They also tend to slow down sexual stamina.

We're Never Too Old for Lovemaking

 No matter the age, it's normal to engage in intimacy with flesh to flesh, sexual lovemaking. It can become even better, although perhaps not indulged in as frequently. Less can be best if it's done right. Older people can relax and enjoy the quiet glow of mature intimacy that goes beyond the hot burning passion of youth. It can still be just as romantic and spiritually satisfying. Even orgasms can be felt deeper.

People are never too old to yearn and never too old to learn how to have great sex. There is no shut-off age for sexual outercourse or intercourse. Some people have hotter sex in their sixtees and seventees than they did when they were sixteen and seventeen-year old-teenagers. They have less to worry about. Pregnancy is no problem and their parents aren't around to tell them what they can't do.

In a survey conducted among men aged 18 to 50 years, it was found that the length of time men could maintain an erection varied from five minutes to an hour. One of the startling facts revealed is that while there is a tendency for the length of endurance to diminish with age, this is only in relation to the individual man's original capacity for virility. For example, a man who as a teenager was able to maintain his erection for an hour might still be able to sustain the erection at age 65 for fifteen minutes or more.

On the other hand, another man, whose erection lasted fifteen minutes as a youth, might be reduced to perhaps three to five minutes. While one cannot realistically expect an older man to have the stamina that he did as a youth, one can expect that he will be a much better lover by this time in his life and know how to please a woman. So age is a cop-out for many older men who do not want to risk rejection by proposing intercourse with their wives or lady friends.

Where women are concerned, getting older usually means enjoying sexual intercourse more than they did when they were young. When a woman has passed through her change of life and no longer has a contraception worry, she may become more sexual than she ever was as a young vulnerable person. Many women past 60 and even into their 80's have expressed strong desire and need for orgasmic gratification. If they have had the good sense to hang on to their men, good sex is possible and normal for as long as they live. And if they do it regularly, they will add healthy years to their lives.

Assuming that you were led to believe that you were less than normal in one way or another, just being aware won't bring the change. But applying proper positive reconditioning will. Thoughts become reality if you are persistent. Just as self-deprecating images and words have been repeated and ingrained in the crevasses of the mind, so must positive suggestions take their place.

Unless some vital organ of your body has been removed medically, or you are suffering from some disease that causes malfunction, you can train your brain to put you in touch with your highest power and become more than normal or average. Just as many physical ailments are mental in origin, so is sexual responsiveness and performance.

Normal People Like Themselves

People who are unsuccessful in satisfying themselves romantically and sexually, carry this dissatisfaction around with them in everything that they do, reflecting their shortcomings in the ineffectual lives that they live. When they are self-deceptive and refuse to face the reality of who they are and how they function, they are also unable to relate honestly in other areas such as business, social, and family levels. The sexually fulfilled person projects pride in self and a sense of normalcy in every area of endeavor.

There are only two types of people who are unable to normalize their sexuality. They are:

1. Those who are incapable of understanding.
2. Those who are unwilling to improve themselves.

The next chapter will introduce you to a practical program which will enable you to reach your highest potential, if you are motivated to do so.

Chapter 5

Optimize Your Sexual Potential

- ☑ *Relax each other before sex*
- ☑ *Enhance pleasurable sensation*
- ☑ *Breathing for increased power*
- ☑ *Erotic images are aphrodisiacs*

 While sex is not essential to life, it is like any other luxury - once experienced, it feels like a necessity, especially if you can't get it. Fortunately, the sex drive is pliable. We can train the libido to behave in a routine or wildly ecstatic manner. Erotic behavior is self-regulated. Think of how sex should make you feel, and soon you'll feel the way you think. All feeling is preceeded by thought. There is a circular connection — mind to body and body to mind. Thoughts stimulate the nerves, which in turn direct the blood flow to the sex organs, which become engorged, or tumescent. The sex organs then send back to the brain a message of pleasure and the cycle reinforces itself. Because sex starts in the mind, it is the mind's messages that can make it sensational, rather than a chore or a bore. As time causes passion to cool down, the mind can fan the embers and generate a new level of healthy sensuality.

There are five keys to open up the highest level of sexual love in both men and women.

1. Awareness..Knowing who you are and what you want.
2. Relaxation..Reducing the stress that inhibits.
3. Breathing..Energizing the sexual machinery.
4. Erotic Imagery..Seeing yourself as perfect.
5. Self-suggestion..Changing your inner voices.

Remember that your reconditioning program involves not only the building of good sexual habits, but also breaking away from the old, self-defeating ones.

Keep These A B C's in Mind

A. A fundamental of good sexual response is faith in our ability to function as nature originally intended.
B. No matter how severe your negative conditioning, it can be corrected with applied positive auto-suggestion.
C. People can and do improve at any age and at any stage of their lives.

However, anxieties can interfere, based on negative images planted by forces out of our control. When this happens, the mind-to-body connection is not made. Every man, unless he's sworn to celibacy, wants to be as virile as possible. Yet, virile men are not necessarily great lovers. They have to learn how to be great lovers by training themselves just as they do in other sports. Where women are concerned, passion and erotic sensation may be there but if her mind is shut off, both of them will fail to make a real connection.

The wall of collected blocks of "sensory resistance" have to be removed one by one, to clear the way for the natural flow of sensation from the central nervous system to the genitals. Outside suggestion, when believed and accepted by our minds, becomes internalized as if spoken by the receiver. We then reinforce this negative thinking by unwittingly carrying out the suggestions that don't serve our best interests.

When you have succeeded in untangling the web of negativity tied to the past, your own positive program can help you accomplish the following:

1. Stop the erosion of your body's vitality.
2. Raise your emotional state to joyfulness.
3. Intensify and prolong sensory sensation.
4. Maintain mind-control during intercourse.
5. Prolong the ecstatic release of orgasm.

Traditionally, women have suffered more than men because of pleasure denial. Being up-tight becomes an ingrained habit. Fortunately, habits are changeable.

Motivate Yourself to Change

Remember that motivation sparks and ignites your innate power to reach toward your true potential. Learn to expect more of yourself and you will deliver more. Having discovered what you want and that you are capable of achieving it, set about getting it. There is a simple truth that can help free you for greater happiness: No matter what has happened in the past, right now, only you are responsible to change yourself.

Anyone can correct bad sexual habits by the program outlined here, using visualization with relaxation and auto-suggestion. There is evidence that mental preparation can prime and prepare the sexual organs to carry forth an improved way of functioning. Studies have measured the increase in male erection control and female lubrication in the genitals of men and women who used the mind/body connection exercises in this book. Researchers have known for some time that brain-power can boost hormones and other natural chemicals. Not only must we be aware of how our habit patterns were mapped out in the past, we must be immediately alert to the fact that each thought we think right now is either helpful or harmful.

Get to Know Yourself

Awareness and self-knowledge makes it possible for us to systematically sort out and discard old, negative, defeatist thinking about ourselves and replace it with rational thinking about how our bodies function. Fear of failure is a sure way of making failure happen. Psychiatry points out that worrying about the lack of something brings about that very lack.

While we cannot expect a problem-free love life, we can learn how to accept what we cannot change and gain comprehension to change for the better where possible. In sexual matters, as in all else, we learn by doing, yet practice leads to perfection only if we do not repeat the practice incorrectly. Mastering skills takes us, step by step, to the highest pinnacle of erotic ecstasy. A robust sex life takes more than control of sexual performance. Sexual attraction begins in the crevices of the brain. Putting two heads together and having a meeting of the minds assures the meeting of the bodies will be thrilling beyond original expectations. Sex will never be boring if you practice mental foreplay. You will give a deeper meaning to the expression, "giving good head." Positive minds bring the ecstasy of sexual empowerment.

Coordination between the forces of mind and body give a person a "self-togetherness," that radiates and instills confidence in every area of endeavor. Our human qualities, our talent for creativity gives us extraordinary advantages over all other forms of life, in getting emotional gratification from our lives.

Male and Female Attitudes

There is an important difference in the way a man thinks about sex in contrast to the way a woman thinks about it. Whether male or female, the most powerful motivation for passion is our own thoughts, which arouse us well in advance of actual physical contact. However, for a large number of women, her thoughts are inclined to shut off her *mind-to-body arousal apparatus*. Inbred resistance turns down the dials of her sensory reactors, while his eagerness turns his reactors upward for readiness.

 Men are more in touch with their senses—sight, hearing, smell, taste and touching. They are more inclined to excite themselves because they are open to eroticism. Most men have trained their pleasure responses from their early teens by masturbation. This

has had the result of intensifying genital pleasure. The have trained their pleasure centers before they have the first real sexual encounter with a female. In contrast, most women have been told not to touch themselves and because they have not allowed themselves "self-pleasure" their sensation level has stayed lower than men.

Some women I have worked with as a sex-therapist have problems so deep rooted, that only ultra-depth hypnotic techniques were able to correct the disparity between their conscious desire and the subconscous blocks. In the past, sexual intercourse is over too quickly, once a man penetrates the woman. That doesn't have to be so. It is possible for a man to reach a level of pleasurable sensation and then hold back climaxing to enjoy the plateau. This kind of man and woman have mastered the art of body control by learning "mind-patrol."

Anyone can learn to do this by visualizing what they want to happen. It works based on the fundamental law of the self-fulfilling prophecy: "Whatever you think upon persistently, tends to happen to you, eventually." The first step in mastering mind-control is to adopt an optimistic attitude. Welcome every possible chance to say, "yes" instead of "no." Don't teeter-totter on the brink of every decision with "but," "if" or "maybe." You have to know what you really want, before you can get it. Motivate yourself to accomplish self-empowerment and your reflexes will accept your command.

All physical behavior is based on the conditioned reflex, which is an automatic reaction to stimulation of the senses. If your sexual reflexes have been conditioned to reject sensuality, don't give up. Reflexes can be Deconditioned and then Reconditioned to behave at their optimum best. Habits which seem to be locked in, can be unlocked with the power of the mind. Think about where negative suggestion is coming from. Examine the source and search out its motivation. Know what your true desires are and do not choose to continue a habit if it is contrary to your needs.

It is important for your general health, as well as your sex life, that you be consciously aware that when you experience good emotions, feelings of happiness, cheerfulness, hope, trust, confidence - your body reacts by improving its function. On the contrary, when you feel depressed and moody, or anxious, fearful and guilty, these emotions have a disturbing effect on your body's machinery. You can re-inforce or erase a problem.

What has once been incorrectly learned, is not necessarily permanent. The mind is like a tape recorder which records and erases constantly. Learning to the point of habit pattern is called *conditioning*. Getting rid of the habit is called *deconditioning*. Replacing the bad habit with a good habit is called *reconditioning*. You are doing so, right now, as you read and absorb the ideas in this book.

Every thought you think, every word you speak, brings with it a physical reaction because: Attitude Affects Anatomy. If your words, spoken or unspoken, are "put-downs", don't expect to have your sex life uplifted. Words, your own, or others, can effect the arousing and enlarging of sexual pleasure. Words bring with them an emotional quality which is essential to the fullest release of sensuality.

The sound that has the greatest affect upon us at all times is the sound of our own voice. Notice how your own declaration of positive anticipation affects the degree of pleasure and control that you feel. Say the right things to yourself. You are always listening to the sound of your own voice and are prone to accept your own advice. It is never too late to become better. It begins with knowing who you are and what your own unique potential is. Feelings that have diminished by the mind can be restored by the mind.

The Power of Mind-Control

Many otherwise well-informed women honestly believe that all men are born with total control of the blood flow to the penis. However, mind to body mastery is a skill that has to be developed. Erections can happen accidently, but control over the erection doesn't happen accidentally. If a man is not as aggressive as he was before marriage or before years of living together, a woman wonders if he is no longer excited by her. If she lacks sexual self-confidence, she may assume he is enjoying sex outside of the home.

The wall of collected childhood blocks of "sensory resistance," have to be removed one by one, to clear the way for the natural flow of sensation from the central nervous system to the genitals. Beneficially, nature always strives to assert itself and circumvent the erroneous scripts of childhood. In spite of the fact that a person may be sexually incapacitated by early conditioning, healthy function can be restored and orgasmic capability brought to life, if one sincerely applies the principles described in this book.

Emotions set off imagery in the subconscious mind which controls the nervous system and its arousal response. Thoughts and pictures stimulate the nerves, which in turn propell the blood flow to the sex organs which then become engorged, or tumescent. The pressure of the swollen genital tissues increases sensitivity and expectations of satisfaction. You can turn on the dials of sensory reactors, by taking time to involve all of her senses - sight, hearing, smell, taste and touch.

A man can get an erection in just a fleeting moment, such as when he sees a female whose looks excite him. The erection of the penis requires blood and *it is the erotic thought that directs this flow*. This also explains why women who have trouble climaxing, can correct the inhibitor by focusing and feeling a strong desire. This involves imagery, breathing and corrective autosuggestion.

Rejection of orgasm in thought becomes rejection by the body's autonomic nervous system, which controls all sensation, pleasant and unpleasant. Male passion is directly linked with his process of fantasizing, which becomes entrenched during his masturbatory years. During lovemaking men recreate many of the images that brought them satisfaction in their youth. Women need to develop a helpful fantasy otherwise their minds tend to wander and they lose sensate focus.

Modern scientific literature stresses that the most casual idea has bodily repercussions. Each and every thought has its subliminal, physical follow-through. This dynamic power has been termed "psychosomatic pre-conditioning," which simply means—"If you think negatively, your body will suffer from such thoughts." We know there are two areas of the brain that direct our every activity. One side, the right brain, conjures up the image, while the other side, the left brain, carries the picture through its intricate nervous system and affects the anatomy.

Many people are sexual cripples because they are unaware of this process. The left brain cannot give you sexual satisfaction if the right brain has a diagram of negative response from early training. The disparity between the male and female ability to experience peak orgasmic sensation comes from attitude, not just anatomy. Awareness helps us think rationally with intelligence. As we develop this insight, we begin to realize how vast is the realm of human potential.

Awareness is the Key to Solving Problems

Awareness bridges the gap between knowing and understanding. It allows you to embrace both your limitations and virtues. It enables you to take a backward glance, learn from early mistakes, and feel confident about the future. An awareness of even the most trivial everyday occurrence makes life more meaningful and widens our scope of living in the "here and now."

Every time you think and every time you speak, each thought and word brings with it a physical reaction and a possible effect upon your lovemaking. So start to notice how you feel and what you are doing based on those feelings. An alert attention to what is happening at the moment doesn't take extra time, it is simply woven into the fabric of everyday thinking. While intellectual insight discloses this potential to us, doing something about our inadequacies demands that we also take action to change for the better.

Adding the emotional quality makes the difference between just knowing about problems and making up our minds to do something about it. We can use awareness not only to enhance the present, but to better comprehend the past and its affect upon us in the future. We reach into our memory so that the helpful information that is stored there will come back to us in our need.

Fortunately, we do not have to stay stuck in a rut of negative conditioning. Psychosomatic reconditioning alters the blocks that were set up by the "no's and don'ts", as well as the failures that cut into our confidence. Once we comprehend the law of *cause and effect*, we can use the same principles that caused resistance to pleasure, and develop normal responses.

When people become aware, they discover that they and only they, have the power to release natural feelings. They find sex can be a spontaneous, exhilarating, freeing experience. Where women are concerned, unless the inhibited woman stops depending on her man to perform miracles, she may remain forever trapped in her negative childhood, fenced in by her mother's negative role-modeling.

Unawareness dooms people to a life of vacuous despair. It is like a blind person stumbling to find his way through a dense forest. Not knowing why, they move through their lives as if in a dream, totally unaware of the forces which influence them.

Who's Pulling Your Strings?

Like puppets, controlled by strings tied to the past, unaware people stay in a rut, acting out unfinished business of their own childhood, or what's worse, their parent's childhood. However it's never too late to grow up and enjoy the pleasures of maturity. Just keep in mind, growing takes knowing where you're going. No matter how far we need to travel, every journey starts by taking that first cautious step in a new direction.

That first step is examining who you are and how to change for the better. Self-awareness is the "do-it-yourself" analyzer of past experience. It transforms sexual confusion to clarity. Every time you think and every time you speak, you should know that each thought and word brings with it a physical action and a possible effect upon your body.

Much of our involuntary physical activity is a result of ideas planted in our minds a very long time ago. This is especially true of our sexual activity and unless the obsolete messages, which we are apt to keep receiving, are cancelled out, we cannot hope to reach our goal of full sexual potential. You must decide for yourself between a negative or an affirmative way of life. And then do something concrete about it.

If you "program" yourself by combining all five steps described here, into a complete reconditioning period and stick to it regularly, the results will astound you.

Notice the slightest improvement, nurture and encourage it within yourself. Practice being definite, positive and decisive in every avenue of your daily living. Lev Tolstoi, the famous Russian author and philosopher said, "Whatever you are in the bedroom, you are in every area of your life." Improve sexual function and the rewards will be manifold. Don't make a ponderous problem about sexual function.

Learn the facts and face problems with courageous insight. Letting your mind stew in a quandary only serves to make stronger your inability to use it as a strong directing force for your body. Don't be afraid to move forward against the current; that's how we become stronger, by overcoming the obstacles that life has put in our path.

Introspection has unlimited power, both positive or negative. If your thoughts are of a defeatist nature, you are surely going to defeat yourself. However, if you think and speak as a winner, you cannot help but win out over adversities. Your wondrous brain is constantly exercising control over both the involuntary and voluntary systems of your body. It determines all of its action based on recordings of past suggestion. What are you telling yourself, verbally or silently? Awareness gives us the independence to reject those ideas that do not fit into our self-image. Once you are aware of wanting to change and have set a goal for yourself, the next essential is motivation toward the cause for which you are striving. Determination is fired by emotional desire. And nothing is more emotional than the desire for sexual fulfillment.

Suggestion is either positive or negative and has unlimited power in both directions. If your thoughts are of a defeatist nature, you are surely going to defeat yourself. However, if you think and speak as a winner, you cannot help but act like one and recieve the rewards that you deserve.

Bring out the best in your partner. Exchanging optimistic attitudes helps develop intimacy. Webster's dictionary defines Optimism as "The doctrine that the good of life over-balances the pain and evil, the inclination to put the most favorable construction upon the actions and happenings, to minimize adverse aspects, conditions, to anticipate the best possible outcome, to have a cheerful and hopeful temperament."

When you discover how your mind thinks you will, at the same time, discover how your body responds to your thoughts. Many things cause stress, but negative emotions head the list: fear, anger, jealousy and vindictiveness. A host of other emotions wreak havoc with the body's nervous system. Unless a person knows how to throw off this burden of accumulated tension, it can cause breakdowns, both physical and emotional. On the other hand, a positive, optimistic outlook is a direct aid to maximizing a pleasurable intimate life. You can zap tension and zip up to the zenith of who you really are. Fulfill the high minded, physically perfect person that nature and God intended for a member of the most intelligent, evolved of all living things on this planet.

If your behavior has been self-harmful rather than self-helpful, take heart. You have the power to alter your responses by building an "umbrella of awareness" as a shield against the constant downpour of pessimistic input. Most of us become so accustomed to accept other people's evaluation of ourselves, we turn over our neuro-transmitters and become manipulated like a robot. Begin to notice what's happening around you.

Noticing even the most trivial everyday occurrences makes life more meaningful and widens our scope of "here and now." Awareness of what is happening at the moment doesn't take extra time, it is simply woven into the fabric of existing activity. It's a state of mind. We can use awareness not only to enhance the present, but to better comprehend the past and its affect upon us.

Life without awareness relegates one to an aimless existence, manipulated by outside forces, like flotsam and jetsam on the shores of time. Awareness gives us control-power to choose the kind of life and lovestyle that brings the greatest fulfillment. Much of our involuntary physical activity result from ideas planted there a long time ago. Unless obsolete mind messages are cancelled, we cannot hope to reach new heights of happiness. Now that you are more aware of your power, let's take the next step, which will open up the channels from mind to body.

Ultra-depth Relaxation

The root of the word *Relax* comes from the Latin, *Laxare*, which means to let go. When a man tells a nervous woman "Just relax and enjoy it," he is repeating what his forebears have said since the beginning of time. Without the use of relaxation techniques, the process of sexual reconditioning would take a long time and might prove discouraging. Relaxation speeds up the process of retraining the reflexes to relax and release the accumulated stress which exerts muscular constriction. Every tension-ridden muscle or organ represents emotional conflict left unresolved.

Relaxation for Pleasure Enhancement

1. **Select A Time Of Day.** The best time is usually just before falling asleep or first thing upon awakening in the morning. Twice a day is twice as good.
2. **Pick A Comfortable Place.** Familiar surroundings increase a sense of privacy. Make sure no one disturbs you. Arrange not to be interrupted by phone calls.
3. **Loosen All Clothing.** Remove shoes, belt, tie, glasses, contact lenses, (or bra, if you wear one) and anything which might restrict your rhythmic breathing.
4. **Settle Into A Comfortable Surface.** Experiment with pillows. Some people like to tuck one under their knees, thighs, or neck. Some people prefer to lie flat on the floor.
5. **Check Your Body For Balance.** Arms should hang loosely on each side, palms upward. Separate your legs and bend your knees slightly.
6. **Think "I'm A Limp Rag Doll".** Let yourself go like a marionette dangling on a string. Think of the joints of your body — shoulders, knees, and hips as loosely connected.
7. **Gently Close Your Eyes.** Let your eyes roll up inside your head as if you can look into your mind and see your relaxed body. Eyelids softly caress the surface of your eyes.

Once you have learned the methodology described here, you will be able to use it for many purposes in addition to improving your sexual pleasure. You will fall asleep easier and sleep more soundly, as well as cope with the tensions of people you come into daily contact with.

Routine to Use Before Sex

When your body is adjusted to as comfortable a position as you can manage, forget about it for the time being. (I suggest you put this tested routine on audio tape and play it to yourself before sex.) Visualize a limp rag doll tossed on a soft bed. Tell your muscles to just let go. Pause for a moment. Notice a general looseness throughout your entire frame. All the joints of your body are limp, like a puppet on a string, dangling aimlessly. Think of melting the large muscles of your body. Think warm and melting.

Set all thoughts aside. Postpone decisions. Leave judgments to another, more suitable time. Slip into your inner quiet core. Enter your center of bliss. Let conscious perception of time drift away. Feel yourself in the moment - here and now. Launch your mind into another space away from mundane reality.

Next, loosen clothing which might restrict or hamper you: buttons, belts, tie, girdle, brassiere. Remove shoes, glasses, jewelry, and anything else you wish. Now, settle down into a comfortable position with your arms resting loosely at each side, palms turned up, elbows softly bent. Your legs are separated and relaxed, knees slightly bent, with toes pointing in opposite directions, Yoga style.

Think only of how good it feels to release the body of tension. Postpone decisions. Leave judgments to another, more suitable time. Take into yourself an inner quietness. A peaceful sensation spreads through your mind. Conscious perception of time drifts away as you relax all over. Notice that your breathing has slowed down. Place your hand on your lower diaphragm and monitor the rhythm of your breathing.

Now focus attention upon your eyelids. Slowly and softly close your eyes, like a flower closing its petals at the end of the day, having seen enough of the bright sunlight. Rest your eyes, for the resting eyes rest the mind and the resting mind rests the rest of the body.

Next take three deep breaths as you think to yourself, "I am breathing in relaxation and breathing out tension." (The next step will give you detailed instructions on how to develop sexual power through directed breathing, but for now, just breathe deeply.) As you continue to breathe deeply and slowly, think of your entire body as very loose.

Starting with your scalp, direct a soothing thought into each area of your body; a loose, limp feeling of easiness. Think to yourself, "My scalp is loose, limp and very relaxed. My forehead is serene. My entire face is smooth like a newborn baby." Visualize the expression on your face as it reflects inner peace of mind.

Focus direct feeling into the tissue and nerves of each part of yourself. Silently say to yourself, "My cheek muscles are loose and relaxed, the hinges of my jaws are open, lips barely touching. My teeth are apart. My tongue is resting in the lower part of my mouth. I feel so soft, so limp, so free. So comfortable. I feel sensations of warmth and pleasure flowing into the center of my body. I can see the blood flow. It is deep pink color, flowing into my sex organ, throbbing, tingling with feeling." (You will also add breathing, visualization and suggestion described in the next pages.)

Continue talking to parts of your body: "My neck is relaxed and the shoulders feel heavy. My arms feel heavy, loose, limp and deeply, completely free of tension. I am breathing slowly and rhythmically and my entire chest and torso is relaxed. My hips feel heavy, buttock muscles melt into the heaviness. My thigh muscles are relaxed, open and heavy and my knees are loose."

Let the loose, relaxed feeling drift from your face through every part of your body. Ask yourself if you are holding back in some area. We all have chronic muscle spasms which shut off circulation and limit sensation to the sexual area. Once your body is generally relaxed, you are ready to concentrate on sexual improvement. Think into the muscles and nerves a feeling of easy moist, warm openness. Focus on a feeling of freedom as you let every part of you go, deeply and completely limp.

Continue the self-talk. "Now my feet let go, they feel heavy, loose, and limp. Toe by toe I let all tension go. Now my entire frame feels completely limp and loose, from the very inside of my bones to the outside of my skin. I feel no tension, just a feeling of well-being."

Keep thinking, visualizing and silently speaking to yourself, "Now my feet let go, they feel heavy, loose, and limp. Toe by toe,

I let all tension go. My entire frame is completely relaxed from head to foot." Imagine a soothing massage just where you need it the most. Instruct your imaginary masseuse/masseur how and where you want to be touched. As you think looseness, let tension go from the entire back of your body, up to the back of the legs. Focus on a free feeling that extends and expands up the back of the thighs into the lower back. Feel the base of the spine let go, and then a looseness throughout the spinal column, as if each vertebrae were wide open, allowing cool, soothing air to pass through, unhampered by tight muscle pressure. Let your spine go, let it become part of whatever it is resting on. Feel the contact as your spine blends into the friendly support of your bed, underneath your shoulder blades.

Think of your shoulder blades as two doors and open them wide and let a pleasant loose feeling into your entire back. When you open the doors of your back all the tension goes out and tranquility creeps in. Let it happen.

To relax even more, now stop thinking and just feel. Empty your mind of all conscious direction. Problems bring with them the tension of making decisions, so let them float away. Suspend, postpone all judgments. Lay them aside. Problems can wait. Let a quiet feeling pervade the inside of your mind as you breathe slowly and rhythmically.

Breathing for Stamina

Breath is life, and to live fully one must learn to breathe that way. Proper breathing is a dramatic aid to sexual power and a natural ally of relaxation. Oxygen increases and releases energy, and sexual activity demands an extra supply above the requirements of normal breathing. Be consciously aware of the depth of your breathing throughout all the prescribed exercises. The slower and deeper you breathe, the better for you. The pressures of daily living cause many people to lose the natural rhythm of their breathing and this shows up in loss of stamina during lovemaking.

Place your right hand on your lower abdomen. (About midway between the end of your rib cage and the navel.) Observe how you breathe in and breathe out. Check to make sure that you are not moving the chest muscles. Remember, only the lower abdomen moves, not the chest and not the shoulders. They are immobile.

Focus awareness into the area beneath your navel. Notice how the lower diaphragm muscles push out as you fill your body with air. Now pull your abdomen in and force your lungs to expel all the air slowly. You are now mentally in touch with your respiratory system. Feel the heavy ropes of muscles on both sides of the spine become loose and limp, allowing the feeling of air to pass through the entire spine, soothing, easing and pleasing every nerve in your body.

Not only is inhalation important, exhalation is also extremely pertinent to sexual fulfillment. The outgoing breath must at all times be sufficiently strong and forceful so that it expels not only carbon dioxide and impurities, but accumulated tension as well. As you exhale imagine the air going out of your pelvic area, taking with it accumulated stress from your genitalia.

Every athlete knows the importance of dynamic breathing for sustaining energy. The long-distance runner trains himself in advance to bring more oxygen into his body for greater energy. Preparation is a keynote of success in sex as well as in all other endeavors of personal enrichment. Planning, training, and preparation are all essential to the winner in any activity. Sexual success ranges from total incapacity to magnificent control, and the manner in which you breathe strongly determines your position on that scale.

Check yourself. Notice how you breathe both during the normal course of the day and during sexual excitement. Are you breathing "with your chest," or are you involving the large diaphragm muscles in the lower part of your torso? These muscles extend below the navel and run around the center of your body. They affect not only the amount of oxygen that you bring into your lungs but diaphragmatic breathing, which helps sexual function in the following ways:

1. It purifies the blood and increases circulation to the penis and to the vulva.
2. The rhythmic respiratory vibration calms the entire nervous system and reduces anxiety.

3. Breathing with the body's total capacity restores and revitalizes sexual energy.

How to Breathe During Foreplay

Anxiety tightens up the body and results in shallow breathing. Shallow breathers cannot help but be shallow lovers, because it takes a lot of respiratory action for sexual energy. Rhythms of breathing change during the various stages of sexual intercourse, but at the onset it should be slow and easy. This gives the woman a feeling that she's not being rushed, that he's confident, and controlled. When a man is over anxious, he tends to breathe in a panting fashion through his mouth. If this occurs before a woman is ready for his level of passion, it succeeds only in turning her feelings down. She feels lost in the high-speed race toward climax, when she would have preferred a leisurely stroll through the garden of erotica.

How to Breathe During Intercourse

Now the tempo speeds up, but it is consciously controlled by the lower muscles. High, nervous spasmodic breathing constricts the entire musculature of the torso and puts one out of touch with the vibrations of the partner. Train yourself to fill your lungs in one smooth movement and expel the air in the same way. You will be rewarded by improved feeling, both physically and emotionally.

Approaching orgasm, the breath is now quickened and air is coming into the lungs through both the nose and the mouth. This happens without deliberation, without effort. It helps the body sharply increase its intake of oxygen for the expenditure of energy about to take place. To prolong the orgasm, try the following: As orgasm approaches, focus away from your sexual organ and upon your breathing. Take a deliberately deep breath and hold it for a moment and think of your power to maintain and sustain the blissful ecstasy of prolonged sensation. This will prepare you for the eventuality of spiritual sex, which will be the final culmination of your training.

Here's the secret: As you breathe in through your nostrils, imagine that the air is passing through the inside of your body and out through the opening of your penis (or vagina). This is a mental-control device and helps to condition the sexual reflexes. You will feel the power of expanded sensation as you take a very large breath and then, very slowly, exhale as you drift into the release phase. It helps if you pace the rhythm of breathing.

Here's how: Breathe in to the count of five. Hold for one or two counts and then breathe out slowly for the count of five. Next, rest for five counts and start all over again. There are four distinct stages in the sexually energizing breath:

1. Inhalation.... 5 counts
2. Pausing......1-2 counts
3. Exhalation.....5 counts
4. Pausing..... 1-2 counts

The count of five is an easy tempo to establish as a beginning exercise in developing sexual control.

You can also gain greater stamina by increasing the count in the following manner: Ten inhaling, five hold, ten exhaling, ten hold. This is the basis for Yoga power breathing and is very beneficial for your health, as well as the source of powerful sexual energy.

Proper, deep rhythmic breathing activates the entire body, internally and externally. (The tempo of the bellows-like action of the lungs also influences the nervous system.) The lungs in motion massage the organs of the body. Have you ever noticed an animal in repose, how his abdomen rises and recedes with each leisurely breath? That is relaxed breathing from the lower diaphragm (something most humans have forgotten how to do).

How To Breathe To Maintain Erection

Premature ejaculators are invariably shallow breathers and can be greatly helped. Ancient erotic literature describes a method of "genital breathing," which is a wonderful aid for overcoming nervous tension. It is a method used for thousands of years in "Tantra Yoga,"

for focusing on erectile control for men and pleasure enhancement for women. Anyone in normally good health can learn to do this.

As you breathe in through your nostrils, imagine that the air is passing through your nostrils into your brain, gathering mind-power which you send with the breath through your body and out through the sex organ. This is a mental-control device and helps to condition the sexual reflexes. "Genital breathing" works for both men and women. It is a wonderful aid for overcoming nervous tension by sensate focus away from the area of anxiety. For men it is directed toward erectile control and/or difficulty in releasing orgasm. For women, it will increase sexual sensation inside the vagina and make the orgasm stronger and responsive to penile penetration. Women who hold their breath during sex, and many do, will find these techniques especially helpful.

Erotic Image Meditation

Humans have an extra ingredient other forms of animals do not possess. That ingredient is creative imagery. Mental images form blueprints for the body to follow. By applying the proper visualization, you enforce the law of the self-fulfilling prophecy and change yourself for the better. It is not magic. It is science of the mind.

When you see yourself as completely responsive, you become what you always were capable of being. Mental images affect the body's anatomy. If you visualize yourself as sickly, you tend to become that way and vice versa. See yourself as basically strong and you will become stronger. Harness improved self-images to improve body function. We react erotically by a signalling system which sends sexual pictures from the brain via the spinal column to the sex organs.

Sensation and increased blood flow are then triggered by the thought patterns and images which flash through the screening area of the subconscious. When the images, words and thoughts are positive the body opens its pleasure center. Don't be embarrassed about exploring, investigating, and experimenting when you reach your pleasure center. Try imagining scenes which might have shocked your mother, or grandmother. Opening up to repressed fantasies can stir your libido into behaving like a super-stud (or stud*ess*). Once you accept your sexuality on a mental and emotional level, you will discover that your body has a natural tendency to motivate you toward sexual improvement.

Your thinking mind is dictator over your sex organs. Male erection, as well as female stimulation, reflect mental images which are constantly flashing within the recesses of the mind. To correct the images from negative to positive begins with a relaxed mind and body. The deeper you relax, the easier it is to reach inbred scripts that probably need changing. With persistence you can erase every trace of negative imprinting from your brain. With the clarity you will gain, a whole new way of love can become a joy for you and your partner.

Erotic Images Act Like Aphrodisiacs

Foreseeing is conceiving, believing—and achieving! Once you have entered a tranquil mood you have set the stage for creative, constructive meditation which enables one to improve genital responses. Acquiring this ability takes some concerted practice but you will find it well worth the effort. The best sedative for the entire human body is meditation that leads to shared sexual blending. At its best, it becomes spiritual. That is the final reward for your effort. Only recently have scientists discovered why erotic meditation increases sexual pleasure. In the past, we knew that meditation relaxes the body and soothes the mind, but there was no scientific proof as to why this happened. Now we know.

The answer lies in the fact that meditation increases the flow of endorphins, and other natural chemicals, manufactured by the brain to combat tension. These endorphins relax nerve endings and improve bodily responses. Orgasm resulting from such sex can be so therapeutic that emotional problems disappear along with the stress. Anxiety vanishes as the body and the judgmental mind are transcended. Once you are so relaxed, breathing deeply and focused mentally, let old memories flow away. If images of negative sexual experiences come to mind, dump them like garbage, which serves no useful purpose. Positive images will take you closer to your sexual potential.

During meditation, you will purge your mind of negative thoughts, untie mental knots and relax the entire nervous system. After a while, banishing negative thinking will become automatic and energize your life in every way. Without periodic respite, the "electric wiring" in your mind gets short-circuited. Emotions become depressed and mental function cloudy. The body and personality become lackluster and you lose the glow that can only come from the build-up and release of mental energy. People who do not have a method of meditation become victims of environmental pressure and are prone to both physical and mental breakdown. Erotic images have a rejuvenating effect because they give the right brain a map of youthful vigor that prevents the deterioration of the hormone system.

Here's an Example of an Erotic Image

Think of yourself lying nude on a soft white blanket at the beach, under a large white umbrella. You listen to the swishing sound of the waves lapping against the sandy shore. Your lover approaches with a cool drink. You recline side by side and stroke each other. Think of fluffy puffs of white clouds on a blue summer sky. Let thoughts, like clouds, drift aimlessly by, blown apart by shifting summer winds.

Visualize each thought, like a fluffy cloud, losing its shape, becoming wispy and melting, dissolving into the blue of the sky, into the tranquil blue of your resting mind. Now imagine you and your mate floating on a large air-pillow, on the surface of a tranquil lake. Imagine the gentle rippling of the water, rocking your bodies as you wrap arms and legs around each other. Let all extraneous images pass by as if they belonged to someone else. Don't claim any conscious thinking. Just tune in to the feeling of intimacy with your lover's body. Picture; imagine rolling and rocking with the waters motion. Visualize yourself in the throes of passionate lovemaking. Take your mediation as far as you desire. Visualize receiving oral stimulation. See yourself returning the pleasure.

Wishful thinking becomes reality when you learn to use fantasy, imagery and self-prophecy to create your own pattern for improvement. Possibilities are boundless for reshaping life through the power of creative imagination.

When you discover how your mind visualizes, you will at the same time, discover how your body responds to that vision. Develop a truer sexual self-image by becoming fully informed as to how your mind impacts on your body. When you accept yourself on an imaginary level, you will discover that your body has a natural tendency to follow along with the improved self-image.

Pre-meditation is the art of planning. Most of us are aware of meditation but few realize the power of pre-meditating for improving sexual fulfillment. A more rewarding application of "thinking in advance of action," is to plan for future sexual experience that improve pleasure performance over the past. This is the most positive use of imagery a person can make. Positive sexual suggestion builds hopeful expectations on a subliminal level, which later triggers the actualization, automatically. Images stimulate perception and prepare the body for action, and the absorption of positive suggestion.

Positive Auto-suggestion

Your brain, a complex two to three pound, jelly-like structure, is responsible not only for every body function but sexual normalcy, as well. Auto-suggestions are self-commands. If they start the mind and body moving up to higher level of satisfaction, they are the right kind of suggestions. If they are negative, they can take you down to the pits. They are the activators that bring about affirmative improvements.

Not only are self-suggestions self-commands, they are also builders of self-worth, self-confidence, and self-love. When you practice positive auto-suggestion you are deciding how you want to be. Self-suggestion can, if used properly, impart a new depth of meaning to even the most mundane things. In sexual matters, it makes the difference between function and dysfunction.

The fundamental task of your self-persuasion exercises is to establish the connection between your mind as director, and your body as the performer. Self-suggestion can be verbal or silent. Some people "self-talk" while looking in a mirror. The best results are when you tell yourself the right suggestions during actual sexual lovemaking.

The Most Important Suggestions for Men

1. I have every thing it takes to satisfy a woman. I can take time to turn her on.
2. I am confident of my body and have no trouble getting an erection when I want to.
3. Each sexual experience is an improvement over the last one because I plan it that way.
4. I have improved my concentration and have conquered premature ejaculation.
5. I have knowledge of the female body and am not squeamish about any part of it.
6. I keep my erection after penetration, regardless of which sexual position I try.
7. I am never nervous around women and come on with confidence in being a great lover.

The Most Important Suggestions for Women

Here is a sampling of self-talk, which has proved helpful to many women who want to enhance sexual pleasure:

1. I am sexually normal. I have everything it takes to respond to the point of orgasm.
2. I enjoy intercourse and am looking forward to increased pleasure each time.
3. Every time I have sex it turns out to be better than the time before.
4. I will not make a struggle of sex. I will let myself relax and enjoy it like he does.
5. I choose to allow myself pleasure because I deserve it as a loving kind person.
6. When I tend to hold back, that will signal for me to let go and feel a burst of great feeling.

7. Orgasmic sensation will be strong, I will let go and give in to the climax.

Spoken out loud during intercourse: "It feels good to relax and enjoy sex with you. I know I am going to have the best orgasm ever. I enjoy how the penis feels inside. I can feel your penis rubbing on the "G-spot."

The best and most effective way to get speedy results from self-suggestion is to be systematic about it. Setting aside a special relaxation time, and being consistent about it, is a sure way to affect changes. Sometimes we have to exaggerate feeling as we give suggestion to ourselves. This is to compensate for the negative subconscious brainwashing we have received in the past. This is the way to erase every trace of past imprint that hampers pleasure enhancement.

In addition to your own positive self-suggestions, always be alert to the kind of suggestions you absorb from others. Outside suggestion, when accepted by our subconscious, becomes your own. *Once a suggestion is accepted and carried out by the subconscious, it begins its urging to be repeated and reinforced. Eventually what was once a simple outside suggestion becomes an ingrained habit.*

Chapter 6

Monogamy Without Monotony

- ☑ *Make the ordinary extraordinary*
- ☑ *Capture the rapture of adventure*
- ☑ *Play sex games where you both win*
- ☑ *Buy toys in an adult sex store*

 Where there's marriage without sexual adventure, there will be sexual adventure outside marriage. After four to six years of making love to the same person, usually in the same way, it's not surprising that inertia may set in. However, you can recapture the rapture, stir up the juices, and get the fire blazing hotter than ever. Playing kinky sex-games will surely spark the embers.

It's worth the effort because having a one-and-only can lead to spiritual ecstasy. People who can stretch to a new dimension don't ever have to worry about competition. Playing the field is foolish when you've got the best at home.

Promiscuity is like a savage collecting pubic scalps - something is missing — the brain. Using mental imagery, the thrill can be revived, revitalized even better than when the love affair first started. Doing some of the touchy-feely, teasing things you did at the very beginning can trick the brain into producing the "love chemicals" that made the early reaction so thrilling. Complacency causes the brain to slow down its hormone flow, and neurochemicals, such as natural Amphetamines — *Dopamine, Norepnephrine,* and essential *Phenylethyamine (PEA).* PEA is the chemical that newly-in-love people have coursing through their veins. It makes the heart sing and the mind go spacey. It's the love potion that's better than any drug.

In addition, the brain sends gushes of a secretion from the pituitary gland, called *Oxytocin,* a love potiom which stimulates powerful sensation leading to orgasm and a sense of satisfaction. Oxytocin triggers that tingling feeling and not only sensitizes nerves endings, but brings on the strong muscle contractions that intensify the release of orgasm in both men and women.

In a study done with men, researchers found that Oxytocin increased three to five times its normal level during the high-point of climax. Researchers believe this may be even more so with women once they are fully aroused, because women express more emotional feeling. Early infatuation also spurs this burst of erotic energy. Unfortunately, when the stimulating chemicals slow down, so does youthful passion. The sizzle turns to fizzle and people wonder where the love went. With the hot flush gone, many find their eyes begin to wander.

Fortunately, the rush of chemistry can be re-awakened by tricking the brain with exciting situations. This gives you the power to renew the excitement at your will, using the playful games described here. The time for death-defying, sleeping-around, is past. You can have a lot more fun making love at home with your one-and-only. You can do things you wouldn't think of doing with a one-night-stand. If you feel like running around acting like a "wild and crazy guy," take your clothes off and run around naked at home! You might be amazed how it will amuse and arouse your spouse. Be playful! Be spontaneous! Sexual experimentation is infinite. Playfulness seldom happens between strangers on the run. It takes time to discover another person's quirks and fantasies.

Both men and women can have what they want by exploring each other's secret desires and then fulfilling those yearnings by playing erotic games. Laughter lowers barriers. A new kind of intimacy takes over and lovers can extend the fun stage to last forever, keep lust alive indefinitely, by acting out their fantasies.

When youthful spirit is put into sex, the love chemicals are tricked into thinking it's a new thrill.

The time has come for routine lovers to let go of past limitations and enjoy legendary sexual pleasure. What makes sex legendary? *Freedom from fear of new experiences!* Playing sex-games can expand the feeblest sensation to the greatest heights of shared ecstasy. This is the time for a woman to open up to all that she missed in her youth. She must join in the discovery of all the mysterious nooks and crannies of unfulfilled memory. Exploration of sensuality while doing the forbidden is a fine way to shake loose from the drabness of inertia.

Great lovers are passionately curious. If you want to be great in anything, dare to be different. Do the unexpected. Take your lover by surprise. Instead of reaching out for a new mate do something new with the mate you've got. To develop star quality, you need to take lovemaking out of the *Ordinary* and move it into the *Extraordinary*. Variety is not only the spice of life, it is the spice that makes sex sensational. Becoming adventurous is the best way to make healthy sex last for a lifetime. There are hundreds of ingredients that add spice to the love stew; unlimited choices are available.

Men welcome an active woman. She should get off her back and into the act. This kind of woman does not have to worry about her mate cheating. Chances are he would have difficulty finding another as responsive as her. Sexually responsive women are not easy to find. Too many are still wearing the cloak of false modesty which covered their mothers and grandmothers. This re-cycled garbage must be dumped as one of the obsolete myths handed down throughout history.

With *Outercourse* you are both explorers. Discover hidden treasures in each other's body. Express your delight with it. Act as if you are totally obsessed with it — a birthmark, her navel, the texture of her nipples or any other marvelous, individual attribute. Talk to it. Stroke it and kiss it. Then offer yourself as a willing subject to her experimentation and allow her to do the same.

Keep in mind that a good relationship includes humor, imagination, and enough elasticity to allow each person to stretch.

We must constantly enrich each other and ourselves. This ensures that a relationship will become more interesting with time. Open your heart and your mind to adventurous eroticism. This is a time to test your imagination. How many playful ways can you think of to arouse and satisfy yourself and love-mate? I'm sure you will come up with your own variations. Meanwhile, here are 100 ways to make sex sensational:

100 Exciting Ways to Add Fun to Sex

1... **Remember the Beginning** — Set up a scene to re-live the first time you met. Only this time around you're very sure of yourself. Get dressed to look the way you did. Arrange to meet at the same or a similar place. Flirt, but don't give in to each other too soon. Keep up the charade until you meet later in bed. Continue reliving the nostalgia throughout the lovemaking.

2... **Release the Inner Child** — Bring back childlike spontaneity and curiosity. Exchange memories of childhood innocence about love and sex. Ask each other questions. What were you told about sex? What was the first erotic thing you saw? What were your fears? Did you play "sex-games?" Compare notes on the first time you were kissed.

3... **Play Doctor and Nurse** — If you think it was fun as a kid you're in for a big surprise. It's even better when you're bigger and no one says: "Stop. It's not nice." Reverse the parts. She'd like to be the doctor for a change. Let him be the nurse. Play the part of patient with a horny doctor. You can improvise a doctor's kit with interesting instruments, like a magnifying glass and tongue depressor.

4... **Have a Party Just for Two** — Guests are unnecessary. However, lots of presents are always great to get, especially if they are sex toys. And a cake with candles gives you both a chance to make wishes for an even closer relationship than you've ever had before. Play party games. And if you can't agree, the cake is there for a wild food-fight to settle the argument.

5... **Make Love in the Kitchen** — Spend a night in and do some home-cooking. While the food is heating up, imagine how hot you can get! Not only can you make the food tastier by adding spices, you also add spice to your sex. Try new ingredients, a couple of neck kisses, a pinch of buttocks, a handful of breast, and a cup of testicles. After sex, relax and eat the dinner.

6... **Eye to Eye Focusing** — This works great when you're out having a drink sitting face-to-face. Look deep into your partner's eyes, without saying a word for several moments. The eyes often reveal what the lips conceal. The first one who looks away has a secret. Try to guess the secret, and if you succeed, your partner has to do you a favor. Make it sexy.

7... **Send Little Love Letters** — Notes left in strange places can trigger erotic juices when you are separated. Stick it in his/her car, wallet, or even on the toilet seat. If you appreciate something and are embarrassed about saying so out loud, try writing it! This practice goes back to the earliest

lovers who left notes carved on the cave walls to greet their mates.

8... **Confess Your Worst Fault** — Tell it funny. Be light-hearted about it. Confession can break down barriers and build a bridge of trust in each other. Nobody's perfect and we need to accept each other as we are. This is a sneaky way to discover the real story behind your mate's facade. Sharing will bring you a lot closer to perfection, in the eyes of your beloved.

9... **Play Follow the Leader** — Players alternate taking the lead in getting the juices flowing. One of you touches, the other returns the same touch. She tickles his toes; he tickles hers. He strokes her palm; she strokes his. He fondles her hair, she fondles his. This game has unlimited possibilities. Invent strange kisses or new words. Remember "Simon Says?"

10...**Old-fashioned Marriage** — Find out what it was like in your grandmother's day. Dress up in dated clothes and hairstyles. He is allowed to be as macho and as demanding as his grandfather or father was. She can behave like a weak, clinging vine. Acting out obsolete roles makes you really enjoy getting back to modern times and treating each other as equals.

11..**Pick a Sizzling Flick** — There is a wide choice of videos that tell and show from a man's point of view, but now there's something special for women. Now there's a softer take on hard core, video erotica made by women for women. Several companies have produced sex films that are also romantic, much needed by both genders. Check your store for titles.

12..**Pamper the Imperfection** — Find a flaw in your mate. Even the best of us has at least one. Show that particular spot a lot of extra affection. Maybe it's a wart or a wrinkle or some hairs growing in the wrong place. A pimple or birthmark will do. Talk to it, caress it. Make nice. It makes your lover special. And when you finish, open up. Reveal your own imperfection.

13..**Electronic Hi-tech Sex** — Try "Virtual Reality, Inter-Active Sex Television." Computers have joined the erotic action, with data bases, such as "CompuServe's Human Sexuality Program."

An electronic bulletin board gives the answers to sexual questions. Experts discuss everything from fetishes to freakish habits. Watch for new astounding developments. It's what's coming.

14..Create a Shared Fantasy — Express your secret thoughts and repressed sexual desires to each other. Nothing is bad if two consulting adults agree to share it. The fantasy will bring you closer than you ever imagined. One of the most common fantasies is one where you are the center of an orgy, where all celebrity invited guests are there just to please you.

15..Alter Your Appearance — Do a make-over on yourself. If you're blonde, wear a black wig. If you're a man, try a moustache and beard. Wear a strange hat. If your dress style is conservative, go wild. Try looking funky, trendy or sexy. Wear excessive jewelry. Look really different. Amaze your lover. Change your voice. Maybe a French accent?

16..Break the Stay Home Routine — A change of place can turn up the voltage. Have you ever considered an adult motel with mirrors on the ceiling? This adventure will start your blood bubbling. How about sex under the stars? Making out on a camping trip shocks the libido and breaks the sluggish tedium. Stop doing things the same old way. Add surprises.

17..Ask for Instructions — Ignorance is not bliss when it comes to making love. Don't be afraid to ask your partner how you can satisfy him/her. And if you tend to be the student most of the time, how about reading from this book and behaving like the teacher? Or the therapist. What can your mate learn from you? With help from your sexologist act out naughty things.

18..Whisper Sweet Pillow Talk — After you've both shared a mutually satisfying, bang-up orgasm, you may feel wiped out, but this is a great time to mellow out and zero in. This is the most open period of lovemaking, so list the things you enjoy about each other. Build each other's self-esteem, not just as lovers, but as friends who really care deeply.

19..Have Fun Flashing Each Other — If one of you has a raincoat, it really is funny. Keeping his shoes on makes it all look more authentic. She can flash him using a fur jacket or cape. Even an old bathrobe can work if you take your partner by surprise. It makes a great winter sport. Go out to dinner all bundled up on the outside and nothing underneath.

20..Double Bubble Bathing — If you have only have a tiny bathtub, you can get really close. Don't forget the rubber duck. One of you makes a body-chair for the other, who sits between the legs of the first. You can not only wash each other's back but also do a lot of other interesting things. How about using a kid's bubble pipe and amusing each other like children?

21..Play Hide and Seek — Before your spouse comes home, leave a note on the door that reads "Look for me. You can have my body, if you find me." When your lover enters, remain quiet. As she/he looks for you frantically in various nooks and crannies, closets and cabinets, the seeker finds notes which read, "warmer," "very warm," etc, until "hot".

22..Explore His/Her Body — Use a magnify-ing glass to get a close-up of every detail. You'll find the sexual area unusually interesting. Notice texture, color, and pattern of fuzz. Become fascinated with a spot you never noticed before. Maybe it's a dimple where you wouldn't expect to find one. Act obsessed and totally scrutinize places you have always avoided.

23..Read Erotic Poetry in Bed — The most beautiful poems ever written are about love. Try Elizabeth Barrett Browning's "How do I love thee? Let me count the ways," etc. Omar Khyam's "A loaf of bread, a jug of wine, and thou beside me in the wilderness," etc. Discover your own. Some people love English Limericks, which are naughty, satiric riddles. Many are erotic.

24..**Singles Bar Pick-up** — Pretend your partner is a stranger and approach him/her in an atmosphere where single people are trying to make out. Take turns doing the approaching. Be more aggressive than you would normally. If you are the one being approached, give your spouse a hard time. Resist and insult. Say "No." Challenging spurs sexual desire.

25..**Rituals of Affirmation** — Remember the first time you declared your feelings for each other? Do it periodically. Married people might have a mock ceremony with a few close friends. And even if it's a "living-together" relationship, give it more meaning with a love ritual. Create meaningful vows and always praise the virtue of your mate. Build his/her ego.

26..**Love's Secret Language** — When a couple gets to know each other intimately, very few, actual words need to be spoken. A look, a touch can say it all. People who deeply understand each other's emotions, develop a kind of "kernel" language, where one word says a whole volume without outsiders being in on the intimacy. Use sign language to encourage or tease.

27..**Kinky Playful Perversions** — Take turns suggesting to your mate anything you ever were curious or shocked about: Foot fetishes, high-heeled boots, chains. You can simulate, using make-believe piercing using earrings that you attach with crazy glue. Paste stick-on notes with instructions on your body parts, explaining what you want your lover to do to you.

28..**Try Dirty Dancing Nude** — Together, of course! Sexy dances like the Lumbada are very erotic, or dream up your own creative free-style. Dirty Dancing, with its hip-rolling can bring a real rush to places that may have grown a little tired. If you go to places, where other people are dancing, it adds that extra suspense because you are holding back till later.

29..Perfumed Satin Sheets — Try the thrill of slipping and sliding over silky sheets while you are making love. The sheets are available in bright colors, like black and red. Musk adds erotic sensuality, or spray her favorite cologne on the pillows. While you're at it, spray each other's private parts. The essence will turn you onward and upward.

30..After Sex, Exchange Facials — He may not be as expert as she, but he can be taught the art of tenderness. The receiver of the good strokes rests his/her head in the other's naked lap and enjoys the loving tender care. Bend down and soothe tired eyes with kisses. Aromatic oil or cream makes it even move delightful. If you're grateful, a tummy-lick will show it.

31..Halloween is Any Night — Dress up in fantasy outfits just for the fun of it. It's trick or treat night, so be prepared to give something up. This can bring laughter and lust to an otherwise tedius evening. Two ghouls making love can break the doldrums and keep a mate from wandering off howling into the moonlight, seeking other dangerous excitement.

32..Groping Under the Table — This is a great turn-on, particularly if you are out on the town, dining in a posh restaurant among guests who are fashionably clothed and proper. If the tablecloth is long enough to hide the goings on, it will be even hotter, because you can do more. Your conversation is casual. Others have no idea you're being naughty.

33..He's Her Sex Object — Turn-about is fair play! Treat the man like a plaything. He's your property, a silly boy-toy! Something you can manipulate as you please. He's your puppet. Tell him so, in no uncertain terms. Boss him around. Most men like a woman to take the lead and call the shots during sexual intercourse. And the man who doesn't, should learn!

34..Strip Tease to Music — Women have been doing this for ages. Time for both to be inventive. Women can get just as turned-on by a man taking his clothes off, as the other way around. When your male erotic dancer does his body gyrations, breath hard. It helps if his body is worth panting over, but if you love him dressed, I guess you'll still love him undressed.

35..Hot Breathe in Ears — There are certain tribes of primitive lovers on faraway islands who find ear stimulation much more erotic than lip kissing. You'll know what they mean if you try it. Licking the earlobes and breathing hot air into the ears is a quick way to warm up the head, which heats up the rest of the body, releasing natural aphrodisiacs.

36..Run Fingers Through Hair — Toying with hair is very exciting for both spouses. Whether the hair is on the head, chest, arm-pits, or pubic area, it's great to discover the many variation in pattern, texture and color. Feeling your hair being tugged gently while you're being kissed is a new kind of stimulation. Try finding some funny stray hairs.

37..The Humdinger Kiss — The performing kisser presses his/her lips against the lover's mouth while humming a familiar love ballad. There's more to this than kidding around. It is really titillating to feel the buzzing on nipples, eyelids and throat. Eventually, the humdinger kiss will be encouraged to descend and create anticipation of erotic affection.

38..A Cat and Dog Making Love — This is very effective in calming arguments. Use only animal sounds. If you're the cat, purr when it feels good. Hiss if it doesn't. The dog barks. He begs. He's obedient. He growls when he wants more. The cat fights back. The dog chases the cat. They are both panting, and finally exchange very wet, slobbery kisses. Peace at last.

39..Tickling All Over — You can drive your partner wild, so be very careful. Not too much too soon. Start at the soles of the feet and tickle your way up. Sure, we struggle against the feeling at first, but what seems like irritation will turn to ecstasy when you finally tickle the right places, in the right way. Use a pink feather and both of you will be tickled pink.

40..All-night Lovemaking — This takes a special kind of stamina, so pick a night when you don't have to get up the next morning. Don't make love full time. This is an on and off thing. There doesn't have to be climaxing, not even a single orgasm. You have lots of time for cuddling and stroking, Some people sleep while the penis remains in the vagina.

41..Go Back to the Cave — There is a wild man in every modern male and a primitive in every liberated woman. Getting back to the jungle roots frees the tamed spirit. Do it gently with lots of humor. Dragging her by the hair is not included. Clubbing him is out of bounds, but picking her up and dragging him around by his legs or arms is permissible for cave people.

42..Hide a Sweet on Your Body — A bon-bon in the navel works if you have a roomy belly button. If not, try a chocolate kiss, or an M & M. There's also your ears or inside your hair. Even your armpits make great hiding places, if they are neat and sweet. Hide a surprise under your tongue and pass it on when you kiss. Can you think of any place else to hide a treat?

43..Spanking or Being Spanked — We're not talking about smacking, or whacking somebody. Loving baby slaps on the tushy are allowed. You stop when the baby says, "Ouch." Some people find it tends to relax them. Others find spanking brings circulation to their bottom and helps sex. Others say it just makes them laugh. Try it, and see how you feel about it.

44..Excite the Erogenous Zones — Arouse the many erogenous zones. Variations on the theme are endless. Pleasure and gratitude will match your efforts. The throat. The inner thighs. The nipples. The eyelids. The tongue. All offer subtle nuances of sensitized taste and touch. Your tongue is an explorer. It is an experimenter. It is an exhilarater.

45..Belly-to-Belly Breathing — This was considered a healing art in many ancient cultures. Place your tummies together, facing each other, or one on top of the other. The lightest one gets the upper position. With eyes closed, synchronize the rhythm. Feel your hearts beat in harmony. This brings renewal of energy and makes relationships closer.

46..Airing Out Problems — After making love let it all hang out. Communicate. There are some people who, instead of confronting a problem, hold it in. They nurse it, or curse it. With great lovemaking you can "disburse it". Empathy results when you share your concerns with a loved one. When you air it out, it diminishes and bonding becomes stronger.

47..Making Out in a Parked Car — The most important first step is to find a safe place. Even if it's in front of your house, it can be exciting. Be sure to lock the doors and bring a blanket to snuggle under. It will remind you of being a teenager and bring back a rush of feeling. You don't have to "go all the way". When things get too hot, go inside and finish up.

48..Project a New Personality — If you've been too shy in the relationship, become more assertive. If you've been too pushy, step back a bit. You can become a new and better person, if you choose. Be adventurous. If you dress conservatively, become more flamboyant or vice-versa. Changing oneself always sparks added attention from others. Make your loved one notice.

49..**Not a Word is Spoken** — This only works when you have known your lover for awhile. Silence is full of meaning, when fingers are tenderly touching and lips are smiling. Romantic emotions are stronger than the verbal language. Where there's rapport between a couple, the meaning is clear. Silence is the most wonderful expression of mutual understanding.

50..**Body Language of Love** — Watch his/her body talk. Physical movements give away the real feelings, unexpressed. You may be more loved than you think. Do you tend to touch each other when you are talking? Do you sit close on the sofa, or do you prefer keeping your space private? Lovers, even in public, have a hard time keeping their hands off each other.

51..**Listen to Music Together** — It doesn't matter if your taste runs to Rock or Bach. Beautiful melody is a great way to harmonize your moods. Studies have shown pleasant sounds make sex more thrilling. You have unlimited choices. Fast music hastens arousal. Slow rhythm deters climaxing. Combine the two for interesting results. Start with the slow, romantic kind.

52..**Every Day is Valentines** — If you want to impress your lover, try this: Spread a white sheet on your bed. With a red marker or lipstick, draw a big heart. In the center, write a love note. As she/he opens the covers — surprise! After making love, serve heart-shaped cookies and a glass of milk. If you don't have a sheet, write "I love you" on your body.

53..**Make Anniversaries Special** — Married or not, the day you met or made your vows of commitment is an anniversary you should remember to celebrate. Maybe it's the day you first looked across the room and your eyes met and something clicked. Even if you're celebrating weeks or months, declare your devotion by arranging a little trip or tickets to something you'll both enjoy.

54 **They're Playing our Song** — Listen to music together. Decide which song has romantic significance for both of you. Maybe it's the song that was playing on your first date, or the time you danced very close. Pick special lyrics that express the kind of deep feelings that you both shared. Then make a tape recording to give as a gift for your beloved.

55 **Flirting and Jealousy** — Though jealousy can be harmful, there are times when it works well. When a mate begins to take you for granted, a little flirting (if not carried too far) may snap him/her to attention. If you're dealing with the really insecure type, moderate the flirting, but don't give up the idea. Just flirt all the way into the bedroom!

56 **Good Enough to Eat** — Prepare to feast on each others body parts. Whip-cream has been the favorite for years and works for lots of people who aren't on a diet. Also, there's the non-dairy kind if you're watching your calories. How about chocolate pudding, ice cream or frozen yogurt with sprinkles? The possibilities are endless. Don't be afraid to experiment.

57 **Secret Sexual Signals** — Couples can agree on all sorts of private signals, known only to them. It gives them an advantage when they are with other people. If they want to get rid of company and go to bed, one of them might tenderly caress the other's arm. On the other hand, to say "No sex tonight," one might punch the pillow and yawn. Think up your very own.

58 **Keep a Photo Album** — There is something very intimate about leafing through a photo album, and remembering romantic moments shared together. Seeing yourselves as a twosome reinforces the oneness. Always take a camera with you on trips and special occasions It builds your future together by sharing and makes living together more of a family.

59..Sleep in the Spoon Position — If you've never tried this, you're in for a treat. Nothing is as comforting as curling up on your side in the fetal position and being cradled by the warm body of someone who loves you. This isn't just to accommodate one partner. Remember to switch positions and invite your partner to be the inside spoon for special touching.

60..Dressing in Plastic or Leather — Sometimes, wearing only saran-wrap can be a masterful turn-on. For Western types, boots are also exciting, especially if you have nothing else on. You don't have to have a fetish to have fun. A leather belt adds a nice touch to the naked body. If you happen to have a cowboy hat, you could look dashing. Try it, you might like it!

61..Dress as a Sex Symbol — This is a popular turn-on and it never fails. She wears lacy, red or black undies, garter belt, hose, and high-heeled shoes; lots of make-up. He wears tight jeans or "G-string" and an open shirt with jewelry. If he has hair on his chest, it helps to show it. If not, he can compensate with his sexy body language. Pelvic roll is good for laughs.

62..Visit a Nudist Camp — "How can that help?" you wonder. Well, when you look around at all the other people, you'll realize that you've made the right choice in selecting the partner you're with. Seeing the frailty of the human body brings a childlike acceptance of naturalness. Bring dark glasses so nobody can tell you're staring at their private parts.

63..Share Some Raunchy Jokes — Couples can release pent-up tension by having a good laugh together. We know that laughter is the best medicine. Nowhere is this more true than for people who are uptight about sexual intimacy. Togetherness becomes more relaxed when humor is involved. Recall the first dirty joke you ever heard. It's even funnier now that you know what it means.

64..**Praise and Compliment** — Recognize the other person's uniqueness. Make a list of the reasons you love your partner: "I love you because you are considerate of my feelings," "because you take out the garbage," "because you look terrific in your underwear." "I miss you, even before I leave you," etc. Then tape the list on the bathroom mirror, so she/he can't miss it.

65..**Place an Ad in a Paper** — Or rent a billboard (if you can afford it.) Declare devotion for the whole world to see. Then drive to the billboard or present the ad to your mate at an opportune moment. This also gives you an opportunity to hint at some future event, like an anniversary: "As each year passes, I love you more and more." "I thank your mother for your birth."

66..**Plants Can Talk for You** — Give your lover a bleeding heart plant with a card saying, "My love for you keeps growing." Or any kind of plant with, "Make sure you take good care of this. Nourish it with water and lots of love." If you get really ticked-off about something, you could send a cactus plant with a note that says, "Please sit on this and think of me!"

67..**Give Each Other Pet Names** — Pick secret names for each other and for parts of your bodies, to express affection. Many insults are associated with sex, so lovers should counteract this by choosing wonderful words to express the joy their bodies give each other. I know one couple who named the husband's penis, "Wee Willie" and the wife's vagina, "Tiger."

68..**Accept the Other's Quirks** — So what if she/he believes in Ufos, or likes to suck his/her thumb. So what if she/he wants to sleep with the TV on, or take a bath with socks on? And why fuss about how a person squeezes the toothpaste? This is high on the list of peeves. Stop treating uniqueness as a calamity. Accept what you cannot change, and laugh about it together.

69..Positions for Lovemaking — Since the beginning of time and in every country in the world, people have experimented positioning their bodies during intercourse. It shouldn't matter "Who's On top?" Roll around and do both. Creativity can result not only in stronger sensations, but greater intimacy, as well. Becoming flexible opens up great possibilities.

70..Show Good Bed Manners — Whether in bed or any other room in your life, manners do matter. Being considerate means that you care about how the other person feels in relation to your behavior. Crackers in bed, snoring, pulling the covers, monopolizing the television can cause conflicts. So discuss the limits and avoid overstepping the boundaries.

71..Enhancing the Plateau — At the height of sensual feeling, pause and communicate emotional feelings to each other. Let your mate know that your closeness is more than a physical act. Affirming the depth of commitment at this time will add a new dimension to your togetherness. Whisper warm endearments as you sustain the state of ecstasy.

72..The Orgasmic Release — Add a special ingredient as your orgasm starts. Join in a "Mantra," prolonging the sound of "Aaahhhh." Climaxing is more than an animalistic reaction to friction. It is a way of letting each other know that there is trust and comfort in body closeness, resulting in the ability to let go. Releasing the sound of pleasure together is bonding.

73..Flex Your Sex Muscles — Everybody's got them, but few know how to use them. They're inside the vagina and around the base of the penis. This is referred to as "The Kegel Squeeze." For men, it improves staying power, and for women, more sensation is felt in the vagina. If you both flex them at the same time during intercourse, you will be amazed at the added friction.

74. **Surrender to Strange Urges** — Free your libido to explore repressed desires. Make a pact with your lover that you will each be allowed to try far-out, erotic sex at least once. If the mate should find it unpleasant, then it is wiped off the slate of memory with no repercussions. One elderly couple loves to give hickys and imitate vampires. (No blood-sucking, please.)

75. **Secret of Sex Appeal** — Men have long enjoyed submissive behavior on the part of the woman, but rarely will a man submit to female dominance. When they do, they admit to loving it. A submissive male allows the woman to become more assertive, increasing her pleasure responses. He can control the action by giving her directions.

76. **Detective and Suspect** — You'll add mystique when you give the third degree. The crime can be anything from shoplifting to murder. Nothing ignites interest like a touch of intrigue. The suspect doesn't tell everything. Keep some secrets about your past activities. Let him/her try to guess if you're guilty. This will add conflict, which stimulates hormones.

77. **Say "No" Sometimes** — The smart lover knows that too much availability can be a turn-off. Having to work for the reward of sex stirs the love juices. The struggle to succeed is enhanced when it isn't too easy. You don't have to completely reject affectionate advances; simply postpone the sexual part for later. Let your mate wait and work for it.

78. **Ask Magical Questions** — The three questions that not only mend fences but draw people very close are: "What can I do to improve?," and "How can I show you I love you?," and "Where would you like to go for a trip or dinner ?" These questions tell the listener you are there to please, and you are willing to change and make the relationship closer to your mate's ideal.

79. **Out of this World Together** — A hot air balloon ride will thrill you, and give you a chance to feel romantic in an unusual situation. Skydiving is also a unique adventure to stir feelings of danger, that turn into great hugs and body closeness when you land safely. And if you can't find a baloon, how about a helicopter flight?

80..**Outdoor Concert When It's Chilly** — Cuddle together, under a blanket, on a cool night in the country, and listen to your favorite concert, even if it's on tape. This is a precious way to become sensually involved. Listening and touching and whispering is not only romantic, but very arousing for the senses. Privately petting among strangers increases intimacy.

81..**A Quality Quickie Sometimes** — Hurried lovemaking is not always bad, nor is it always engaged in due to lack of affection. There may be a plane to catch or an expected interruption. You may discover that spur-of-the-moment, erotic passion is challenging to your creativity rather than crude. When you've been doing it slow-motion, a quickie changes the pace.

82..**Share a Psychic Reading** — You don't have to take it too seriously (unless this is your kind of thing). However, you may find you have a lot to talk about afterward, and I've been told it can stir up meaningful dialogue for future plans and marriage, especially for the man. If you can't find a psychic, you can always psyche each other out, with Tarot cards.

83..**Hypnotize Each Other** — It's easier than you think, because sex makes you spacey. Entering an altered state of consciousness while in a sexual embrace, can bring a sense of mind and body intimacy beyond anything that you have experienced together. Taking this even further, lovemaking while you remain in a trance state can be a rebirthing experience.

84..**It Feels Good to be Bad** — You don't need an excuse to let your demons loose every once in a while. Too much pressure to do the right thing inhibits us. The repression of resentment can bottle up emotions and lead to serious tension problems. Bad is good when it leads to greater understanding. Say what you mean. Mean what you say. Kick up your heels.

85..Visit an Adult Toy Store — This will cure shyness (if you have any left). You'll also discover the many unusual things that other people are doing to break the monotony of their lovemaking. You can just window shop or if you're feeling bold, buy each other a naughty gift to play with later. Here are a few: Finger or penis extender; Ben Wa balls; Tasty lotion.

86..It's Worth the Money — Either one can initiate the deal. The horny one pays a sum of money — ten dollars seems a fair amount as a fun thing. This works to motivate the less active partner, usually the woman, to become more assertive, and lifts the pleasure level for both of them. If the aggressive one dosen't have the money, the other can lend it to him/her.

87..Fabulous Fair Fighting — Begin by disagreeing and picking on each other over something trivial. This is a battle where nobody gets hurt and both contestants come out winners. Of course, there's one catch. The strongest one must let the weaker one win. Rolling around with your clothes off insures that you'll wind up laughing and loving in each other's arms.

88..Sexercises for Better Sex — Muscle development brings with it body control for more flexibility during sexual activity. Work out together. Try far-out positions while wearing your sweats. Do push-ups to build your chest and arms. Deep knee-bends tone the thighs and buttocks. Stretch your ham-strings for flexible positions.

89..Try Temporary Tattoos — A butterfly in some secret place, or not so secret, if you prefer, gives an intimate sense of sharing something that is very personal. You can also have your names tattooed on each other's butt. The best way to make sure it isn't permanent is to do it yourself, because permanent tatoos are extremely painful to remove.

90..**Holiday Body Painting** — Instead of giving each other the same old greeting cards, you can become the greeting card. You can buy washable body paint in any art store. Add a sparkling glitter and highlight certain parts. The best part is washing it off together in the shower, and getting together for the real sparkling lovemaking later.

91..**The Morning After** — If it's been really great the night before, awaken your lover with kisses — all over the face and any other interesting place that has given you pleasure! Show your appreciation of great satisfaction, by doing something special. Breakfast in bed is always a treat. If there isn't time, helping your loved one get dressed is great, too.

92..**Play a Pocket Prank** — Try slipping something in the pocket or purse of your spouse. It will be discovered at a later time to bring a smile to his/her face, and cause him/her to think of you. If he should find her undies in his jacket pocket during a business meeting, it could take the tension out of his day! Also, she might discover a sex toy in her purse.

93..**Enjoy Good Vibrations** — Dependency on vibrators for stimulation shouldn't be the only way orgasm is reached, but occasional vibration can help a body relax, especially after a rough day. Use while sensually stroking. Check out the many choices available. There are short ones, and long ones. Some are straight and others are curved. They're like a real penis.

94..**Watch an Old Romantic Movie** — Play the characters as you snuggle together. Repeat the lines in the script, and then add your own variations. The Bogart /Bacall movies, or any from that era, are especially conducive to romantic dialogue.   This will be a learning

lesson in how to romance your mate, the old-fashioned way. Remember, romance is having a comeback.

95..Tie Me Up (Loosely) — We're not talking about serious bondage or totally restricting movement. However, soft silk ribbons will do nicely and are non-threatening. This is an exercise in trusting your partner to free you when you ask to be released. Reversing the roles, so the man is tied up by the woman, allows for a feeling of mutual acceptance.

96..Exchange Male/Female Roles — This game is serious and can make a big difference in compatibility. Take a weekend to assume the other's responsibilities and personalities. He becomes her. She becomes him. A good opportunity to see yourself as your partner sees you. You will appreciate the other's difficulties and show more sympathy in the future.

97..Some Natural Aphrodisiacs — The greatest stimulant is the fantasy within your own mind. However, many people swear by the old stand-bys like: Ginseng root, oysters, raw eggs, the liquor Pernod and Yohimbe. There are a host of other esoteric concoctions availble. Some believe the placebo effect is at play. So, if you think it will work, it probably will.

98..Exchange Kinky Underwear — Check out each other's undies and if you have nothing that fits him, go on a shopping spree to find something that will,. Make it really far-out, like leopard skin or a wild print. Dress each other in the new look. Discard the old, shaggy, baggy, boring underwear and parade around for each other's amusement. It's a real turn-on.

99..Treat Your Mate Like a Baby — Everyone needs to coddle, and coo, sometime. He can play mother and change her diaper, as she assumes the infant role. Then switch positions. See how much he enjoys giving up his control for awhile, to be nursed and fed like a tiny baby. It's a re-discovery of unconditional love. It gives one a sense of rebirth.

100.Hot X-Rated Phone Sex — Set up your own private hotline. Whether you are thousands of miles apart or just in the next room, you can drive each other wild, by describing things you will do next time you get hold of each other. And if you're calling from the next room, just pop in and act out your unrestricted, uncensored sweet and sexy dialogue, in the flesh.

After you have played together and released the inner-child, you can take your development to a higher plane, by adding sensory awareness. People generally have a built-in shield over their senses, to mute the tumult which results from constant bombardment of environmental sights and sounds. We tend to automatically protect ourselves from the hypertension that surrounds us in daily life. Unfortunately, by shutting off our sensitivities to outside stimulators, we often dull our senses and become calloused to the affect of our sensory organs.

Problems of sensuality are more prevalent among women than men. Eight out of ten women need to become more aware of their senses. When they are too focused into surface appearance, they are searching for approval from the outside, rather than optimizing their innate, sensual potential. We all know that, "Love makes the world go round," but it's *our sensuality that makes the trip exciting.*

Chapter 7

Share Supreme Sensuality

- ☑ *All five senses stimulate nerves*
- ☑ *Discover your secret hot spots*
- ☑ *How condoms can increase pleasure*
- ☑ *Make your partner ask for more*

 The addition of sensory eroticism makes one relish intimacy with epicurean delight. Love-making soars out of the ordinary and becomes extraordinary when your senses become fully involved. It is not just what one says or listens to, but how one touches and feels, the aroma of a lover's body, the taste of each other's lips. The awareness of sensuality adds artistry to the joy of union. Kissing! Laughing! Touching! Tasting (everything)! Tingling (everywhere)! Any high you've ever known is sea-level compared to the elation that your senses can bring to lovemaking.

How a person feels about a lover can be conveyed by the first touch. The power of seduction is at your fingertips. A man's warm hand can melt a cold woman even when her eyes are shut and his lips are silent. A woman's touch can tell everything that he wants to hear — and sometimes more. We have to start by accepting sensuality as beautiful, rather than sinful. It's important for men to be aware of female sensitivity. When men come on too strong sexually, women may become defensive.

Are there some women who are really "frigid?" It is generally accepted by researchers in this field that most women who cannot enjoy sexual intercourse to the point of orgasm, are probably normal in anatomical structure but are repressed sensually due to their early training. They have shut themselves off to pleasure. Many women live out their entire lives never suspecting they can correct this problem. I have worked with women who have never touched their own genitals, because as children they were told this was prohibited. Once they accept an existence of prohibition, they drift into the kind of self-pitying, self-defeating personalties which we often observe around us, caught in the web of early negative indoctrination.

Our Attitude Affects our Anatomy

Once a woman learns to trust a man, her nervous system begins to relax. She becomes more responsive to intimacy because *his attitude affects her responsiveness.* So does *her attitude affect his performance.* It is the freedom to think erotically without censure that causes the senses of lovers to mingle — to touch and tingle. When both minds are agreeable, they can entwine both of their nervous systems into a harmony of timeless eroticism.

People use only a tiny speck of their sensory potential. Most women suffer from sensory deprivation, because they have been taught to believe that giving full vent to their lusty desires is immoral or "dirty." Women, generally, love being looked at and admired. They spend enormous amounts of money on looking attractive, but when it comes to actual sex, many of them prefer to dim the lights. Being seen but "not seeing" separates them from really communicating with their male partner.

Can women's sensory block be removed so lovers can blend without grinding each other's gears? Lovers can help each other rise above the past and see clearly into the future. Love isn't blind, and neither is it so dumb that two people can't overcome early negative conditioning. Encourage your spouse to ask for what he/she enjoys, as well as dislikes. A thoughtful lover might say: "Tell me how you feel when I make love to you."

Most men are more easily responsive to sensory arousal because early male eroticism was acceptable. A generation ago women were expected to be non-sexual. Fortunately, aware people are transcending these imposed limitations and challenging the validity of obsolete concepts. To ignore the senses, as many people do, is to relegate sex to banality, or the vulgarity of mechanical exercise.

Besides giving you good feeling, your senses are also healing, because heightened sensory awareness stimulates circulation and glandular output. This is especially important to women who complain of PMS (post menstrual syndrome). If they allow sensuality to flourish, they can eliminate a great deal of the residual tension in the pelvic area. Relaxed, sensual pleasure is natural, and doesn't need pot, drugs or alcohol for spacing out. The best feeling is when you enter the center of your senses and optimize pleasure as nature intended.

Men Respond Faster than Women

Men are easily turned on by sight, hearing, smell, taste and touching. They are more inclined to get excited because they are open to erotic things and allow themselves to become aroused from within. Sexual dysfunction will be a thing of the past when both men and women build skills for enriching shared, moment-to-moment sensory awareness. The senses can expand the erotic repertoire and bring to men sustained virility and free women to celebrate their lustiness. The combination of all of the sensory responses is the key to a higher degree of sexual gratification. When you master your five senses, you will be rewarded with the ability to ascend to your sixth sense, the spiritual connection.

A woman's early, inbred training holds her back from these natural stimulators which could assist her greatly not only in her quest for sexual gratification, but to normalize her hormonal output. It's a strange contradiction that women spend so much time trying to look exciting and not enough time exciting herself. It boils down to the difference between being a "self-starter" or waiting for a man to get her passion flowing.

When a woman allows herself to think freely about sexual pleasure, she will invariably increase her level of desire from within.

When she allows herself to openly manifest interest in being erotic, her thought processes will trigger her brain to send the right chemicals to encourage a higher degree of sensate pleasure. The disinterested woman can transform lethargy into passionate energy whenever she chooses. Our purpose is to help both men and women free their senses from the cubbyholes, where they have been stored for too many years. Some people have locked them up and thrown away the key. Time to allow outrageous, opulent physical pleasure to flourish without restrictions. Why? Because it's good for you! You will live longer and suffer less ailments. Before this can happen, most of us need to tap the inner core of buried feelings.

The Path to Your Sensual Center

It is your senses that bring you together with this deep core of inner self, enabling sensuality to become something more than the firefly flash of orgasm most of us are limited to. Orgasm should be the completion of a sensuous outercourse journey into a garden of unlimited pleasuring of self, interacting with a loving person of choice.

"The eyes are the mirrors of the soul," the poet muses, and anyone who has looked deeply into a loved one's eyes knows the truth of that statement. Sight can open the iron gate and allow all of the other senses to flood the central nervous system. If a person likes the way the other looks, they draw closer to find out more about the other's inner self.

Because the first attraction is always visual, the facial expression we see, tells the viewer the state of mind that propells the emotions to send messages through the muscles of the face. A ready smile is the welcome mat we each set out to encourage friendship.

Your mouth tells it like it is. The mouth is our first contact with another human being. The combination of smile, affection and food begins with the first taste of nourishment at our mother's breast. From the very first cry of the newborn infant, the mouth is fraught with feelings, both pleasant and unpleasant. The mouth receives sustenance for life, and because of this, the infant attaches great importance to his mouth. He shows love through his mouth, and suckles to receive food. Tender kisses from his mother's mouth return the emotional feelings of comfort and trust that he is learning to associate with the mouth.

A world of delight awaits your freedom as you open up to the myriad sensations of *smell, hearing, touch, taste, and sight.* Later you will add *spirit* to your lovemaking menu and that sixth sense will elevate your intimacy to an ethereal level and take you "out of this world."

Before we can get to that high plane we need to recognize that we've inherited a strange morality, which has tried to kill our natural instincts. It has deodorized us, shut our eyes and ears, and shamed us not to touch ourselves or others lasciviously. We can tear away this false cloak and reveal the naked beauty of true feeling by accepting our natural right to pleasure without guilt or shame. Only then will the mind be free to liberate the body. Sensual liberation brings in its wake an emotional joyfulness that makes life something extra special. It's the secret of happiness.

Give Yourself Pleasure. You're Worth It

One of the basic ground rules between lovers is that anything goes as long as it feels good and doesn't hurt anybody. Lovers grow with each other when they proceed on the assumption that they have what it takes not only to satisfy themselves but to help their partner, as well. An important ground rule is that you must first discover your own level of sensory awareness, for you are your own salvation. If you have "hand-me-down problems" from previous relationships, you must assume responsibility and not expect a new partner to do that for you. No one else can heal you or free your innermost sensuality, so begin right now!

Liberate your eyes. Look, see, observe not only your lover but yourself. Look at both your bodies. Notice the sameness and the difference.

Liberate your ears. Hear, speak, listen, not only to the obvious, but to subtle nuances of sound.

Liberate your nose. Enjoy the exciting aroma of each other's bodies, deodorized and/or natural.

Liberate your touch. Let your fingers freely roam and explore the unexplored areas of wonder.

Liberate your taste. Taste every delicious morsel of each other's clean, sweet-smelling body.

The average person has become alienated from his sensual potential. Some men fear a fully aroused female. Women who have been overpowered by men, are fearful and avoid fully arousing men. So they both avoid confrontation with strong erotic passion. If this applies to you, even in a small way, be assured that you can end this sensory isolation. Any one who chooses to do so, can break out of the dark corner of partial feeling and into the warm glow of full sensory sunlight.

Great lovers avoid quickies unless the woman indicates that is what she wants. People "in-the-know" realize that few women really respond under limiting circumstances. Contrary to the fairy tale of Sleeping Beauty, who was awakened by Prince Charming's first kiss, it seldom happens that way in real life. A wise man knows not to rush, that if he wants her at her best he must take as much time as she needs before intercourse. He must always be aware that prolonged outercourse makes intercourse much better.

In order to bring her up to his own level of readiness, it is often necessary that a man push his own passion back during foreplay and concentrate on building her fire. The big difference between an aroused or unresponsive woman is whether her lover had the patience to give her enough time to help herself get into her center.

The Brain to Body Sensory Connection

Your sensory organs send messages to the brain which relays them to the central nervous system. Your mind can accelerate or diminish sexual pleasure depending on this inter-communication. The subterranean recesses of your mind can send messages through the gateways to every nerve ending in your anatomy. It is the senses that keep the love chemicals flowing from brain to sexual center. Your senses are the tireless messengers that race from brain to genitals via the spinal canal. The nerves in your sex organs then send messages of either appreciation or apprehension back to the brain. The brain then interprets, analyzes, and makes its decision whether this is to be a satisfying experience or a disappointing one.

The troublesome thought may be fleeting, (even one word will do the damage) but once apprehension stirs your spinal cord, your brain sets up its "flight reaction." This causes the pleasurable flow of secretions from the brain to change and the urge is to get away fast. The focus goes away from the sensory system.

The decision as to whether a particular sex experience will be fulfilling or a failure depends very often on what kind of information has been fed into your computer-brain.

The two ideas that often cause problems are:

1. A fear of being hurt physically or emotionally.
2. Feelings of unworthiness. Lack of self-esteem.

The nerve roots that emerge from the brain and distribute their branches to various parts of the body will not communicate pleasure, if you have set up a mental barrier. Not only is your nervous system controlled by your thoughts, your blood circulation is also affected.

The brain uses its "telephone system" to send its communications back and forth to the sexual organs. The central avenue of transportation is the spinal canal that houses all the body's facilities for responsiveness. Sight, sound, smell, taste, and touch deliver to the spine their reactions, the mind picks it up, acts as a scanner, and then directs the next move.

It is the freedom to think erotically without censure that causes the senses of lovers to mingle — to touch and tingle. When both minds are agreeable, they entwine two sets of sensual vibrations into a harmonic blend of shared pleasure. When directed properly, your senses become more than "feelers," they can also act as "self-healers." Your senses can tie broken emotional cords, connect missing links, and make the weakened body as strong as nature originally intended.

Always think of your five senses as five switches that can be reversed from "No" to "On". Your mind can deliberately trigger the switches one by one or all together. When you master the process, you direct your autonomic reflexes to alter their responses from negative to positive. You will learn how to combine all the energy forces of your five senses to work for positive results. The electric high will astound you!

Most people live throughout their sexual lives without any awareness that they have the power to maximize their natural erotic powers. They are not in touch with the latent brain power waiting to bring them the ultimate joy.

The Sensuality of Sight

We are what we think, and we think as we do based on the information submitted through our senses. The Journal of Sex Research informs us that of the five senses, our sense of *sight delivers the strongest message.* Sight transmits 84% of all the information brought into the brain. Sound brings in 10%, and the others make up for the rest. More than any other faculty, it is sight that determines our attraction to a sex partner. The importance of the visual impact of seeing a lover's facial expression during lovemaking, combined with the sound of soft and loving words, starts the chain of brain-stimulation.

Because vision is a powerful message conductor, therefore it can also be a sexual deterrent if what one sees is not conducive to arousal. Women are especially sensitive to the way things look. Therefore, a man should respect that sensitivity and make himself as clean and attractive as possible. He should try to keep his body lean and well-exercised, for both of their sakes.

A sexual experience starts with the first lingering glance exchanged between a woman and a man. Somewhere, deep in the recesses of her mind, a woman knows if she will eventually make love to this man. Biological awareness, that animal instinct, shows in the special way that she looks at him. A prolonged glance is a subtle way of communicating even at a distance. It opens the way for the other senses to enlarge upon the initial reaction to another person.

When glances meet and two lovers look searchingly into each other's eyes, desire is immediately intensified. Eye-to-eye contact reveals the mutual depth of passion. It is, also, a powerful way of communicating non-verbally during lovemaking. The insistence of some women for total darkness can rob the relationship of this subtle method of male-female interaction of desire. Women who have difficulty reaching orgasm often have difficulty looking at the sexual act. They carry over into the sexual act an aversion to seeing themselves doing something which was once called, "not nice for a girl to do." When women cling to this outmoded barrier they lose something that is very important to the realization of full orgasmic satisfaction. They lose an affirmative sexual image of themselves. Seeing one's self having sex and enjoying it, increases the expansion of the senses. So take a good look, don't count your sense of sight out of the picture.

Men are very visual — they love to look at the nude female form. This is in sharp contrast to the way women feel about looking at the nude bodies of most men. Many shy away from the experience, cringing at the thought of looking at the male genitals. This is a hangover from the early suggestion that there is something threatening and distasteful about the penis.

Sexually liberated women need to abandon prudishness once and for all and let the sight of the male body entice desire. A softened light, rather than complete darkness, can be of great help in arousing a woman. When a man looks at a woman's body in candlelight, as a good lover, he assures her she is beautiful all over. If he can get her to look at his nude body and enjoy what she sees, she will be along the path of freeing her innate desire and rise above her inhibitions.

We are all influenced by what we see. The sense of sight always takes precedence over what we are told. "Seeing is believing" and "I'm from Missouri, show me," are the kind of old American sayings that we have grown up with. One reason that some women react negatively to their sense of sight during sex is because they have been conditioned to expect perfection. Some expect their lover to look like Mr. Universe.

Let's face reality. If he/she is less than stimulating visually, by all means, dim the lights. But, if the opposite is true, if looking at him/her turns you on, rather than off, look your lover over and enjoy what you see.

Your expression of pleasure can convey what you might not be ready to say out loud. Your face has an infinite vocabulary of emotion that can only be appreciated when your lover can see how you feel and see how you are reacting to lovemaking. The same is true for him. If you look at him, you may learn much more than just the meaning of the words he is saying. Seeing and being seen lends an air of excitement to lovemaking that starts the other senses flowing and assures a strong orgasm.

Sounds of Sexual Passion

Unpleasant, discordant noises are constantly invading our sensibilities and prohibiting natural relaxation. Our sound waves are polluted with automation's hums and buzzes. Cars, subways. garbage trucks, and the many other screeching sounds of modern life. The best thing one can do is to retreat from this sensory onslaught and listen with a loved one to the melodic sounds of soft voices and beautiful music.

A couple, who were clients of mine, decided after considerable experimentation, that a combination of three records suited their needs best. Perhaps this will prove helpful for you, also:

The first selection is a soft melody. It is romantic for the foreplay and a massage. This is the kind of rhythm that helps you mellow out.

The second is a faster and more intense pace, used for stimulating and stirring up lots of feeling leading to the sensual plateau.

The third, a strong staccato in tempo, would signal the body's vibrations to bring on the rush of orgasm. Ravel's Ballero is a favorite for many.

The Sound of Words

Lovers do not necessarily communicate through the meaning of words. Words are the least important part of sensuous sound. Hot, warm breathing has a special sound of arousal. One can breathe "I love you" in any language, yet the meaning is clear. The vibrations of sound carry  with them an emotional feeling that is more basic than semantics. Try listening to yourself sometime as others hear you. A tape recorder is a great help in this direction. Become aware of how you sound to the person on the receiving end; not just what you say, but the way that you say it.

How about "four-letter" words? Most men tend to think about sex in "four-letter" raunchy words. Very few women do. It's not a question of good or bad — it's just the way it is. If a man is to get closer to a woman instead of having her withdraw, it's usually best to translate his thoughts into more acceptable words that carry with them a romantic feeling. He should watch what he's saying until he gets to know her better. Then her own vocabulary for spicy language may surprise him.

It helps a woman to say "naughty words" that she has never said before. Sound is a powerful force for erotic stimulation. If he is patient, even the most prudish woman will eventually uncover her ears and listen to the meaning of sexual words. Once a woman is aroused, "dirty talk" may help to further stimulate her. On the other hand, if she indicates that certain words are distasteful, accommodate her sensitivity and ask her what would be acceptable to her.

Rather than chance the problem of her being adversely affected by your choice of language, drop the crude words and replace them with romantic ones. There are many women who must be spoken to romantically before they can permit themselves to be physically aroused. The man who isn't aware of this can lose his mate long before mating time.

Some wise lovers invent their own secret vocabulary. When they speak to each other, they send messages of future sexual activities. The also give names to their sexual parts. Try it. It's a fun thing to do.

Vulgarity is only in the ear of the beholder. Get to know your woman as a person before you suggest anything that she may have a built-in abhorrence toward. Eliminate words that may turn her off. Words and sounds can kindle the flame of passion and the right words at the right time can bring a woman to orgasm or shut off all sensation. There is nothing sinful in telling a man to say erotic words that may help you at your peak, but if he gets carried away by his own drive toward orgasm, say it to yourself.

Your ear is a powerful conductor of messages to the brain, and you need that mental directive to reach the peak of climax. The act of hearing takes place when the motion of sound waves vibrates the inner ear, which is in close proximity to the brain. The inner ear is composed of a thin membrane stretched tautly over the end of a tunnel-like structure leading into the brain from the outer ear. The sounds of words make this drum-like structure quiver exciting messages to the brain. The brain, in turn, relays its answer to all the nerves, building anticipation for sexual fulfillment.

The vibrations of the voice, as the words are uttered, give it an emotional quality that stirs imagination. Because the brain is so close to the receiving end of the hearing instrument, every word we say instantly affects how we function. Be sure to say the right words at the right time, not just to your lover, but most especially to yourself through auto-suggestion. Your ears do a lot more than listen to the words that are spoken. They are like sponges that soak up the feeling of sound, the emotions behind the words. As a result of too much of an overload of noise, which surrounds us constantly, many of us learn to subconsciously ignore much of the sound that could bring us pleasure and relaxation.

The need for lovers to communicate is basic to good sexual relationships. Speaking draws people closer and adds a dimension of emotion as one reacts to the message that the ears pick up. What we say and how we say it can build or destroy a relationship. When you think of the three words "I love you" while actually feeling love, you will better understand the impact of emotions on mere words.

Become aware of the sexual sound of your own voice. Even more than music, the sound that has the greatest effect on a person's ability to become passionate and fulfilled is the sound of one's own voice! Most women are embarrassed to talk to men about sexual feelings.

However, when a woman is able to admit that she is enjoying sexual intercourse, she will increase her own level of responsiveness. This is true of the man, as well. Once a person hears his own voice admitting that good things are happening, it causes the good to multiply. That is the power of positive suggestion. You are especially receptive when you are in an alterred state of consciousness, a condition we all go into when in the plateau of lovemaking.

When in this mind-set, a woman says that she is enjoying strong orgasmic sensation, the affirmation will make it become stronger. If a man says that his erection will continue, it will do so. One's own voice is a very persuasive master, and expectations bring their own results. That's why auto-suggestion is so important in sexual empowerment. Passionate love is often possible between people of different languages because of this factor. The soft sound of breathing of a satisfied lover says much more than lengthy declarations of satisfaction.

It is a wise lover, male or female, who makes good use of all of the senses, and in particular the sense of sound because it has a very quick effect on the sexual organs.

Is Our Sense Of Smell Deodorized?

 In spite of the fact that modern culture has methodically tried to do away with all normal sexual odors, there is an animal magnetism that remains on a more primitive level. Each person has his or her distinctive and particular body aroma. Nature designed all species with body odor so that the male and female would be attracted to each other for procreation. Deodorization is one of the many ways that civilization has cut into our natural function.

While all other animals are turned on by body smells, humans are turned off. Big business has made millions of dollars selling scores of products to destroy sexual aroma. No one is immune from the embarrassment of smelling less than sweet. Most civilized people use deodorizing products and it stands to reason that you cannot go against this training if you want a relationship with another person who does use such products.

Television watchers are subjected to tremendous brainwashing. The advertising media constantly campaigns to cloak us with perfumed essences. Because of this powerful conditioning most men prefer a perfumed woman, or at least one who is fragrantly clean. Some squeamish men are horrified by any trace of female sexual odor which can cause them to lose all interest in lovemaking.

Female smell is the brunt of much low-class humor among men. At the same time, hardly anyone makes a point that some men reek of body odor and turn women off even before a second date is contemplated. Nervous tension causes some men to give off a particular pungent odor, especially during intercourse. Some women don't mind and others are repulsed. I know of a woman who visited my office for sex therapy and said she actually divorced her husband because of the offensive odor emanating from his testicles. These days there are products of all kinds to avoid this problem and men should find out about them. On the other hand, I have also heard women say they love the musky, unwashed smell of a man's body. Blue-collar workers seem to be back in vogue.

Passion can be nurtured by aromatic artifacts. Its use is as old as mankind itself. Sorcerers of ancient Egypt and other civilizations compounded complex formulas of flowers and herbs to titillate the rulers of the land. Chemists were in demand for awakening the tired libidos of the royal classes. From King Tut (whose tomb contained fragrant jars of spikenard and balsam) to modern Prince Charlie (and his after-shave lotion) — men know that it helps them with the ladies if they smell a bit sweeter than nature's original design.

Your Sense of Taste

Love usually begins with the taste buds. The very first time a man offers to feed a woman, he is doing something more than just buying her dinner. He is enticing her through her sense of taste to get closer to him, for our sense of taste is fundamentally

sexual. The connection starts at our mother's breast, and continues on until death. We all are subject to a constant association between sexual feeling and taste. In our culture, offering a woman food is usually the first social step in courtship. For both the man and the woman, it pleasantly restores the closeness of mother and child; it satisfies a deep, deep level of hunger.

The same kind of love-food unity takes place when a lover cooks for her/his mate. This restores faith in being loved. That's where the old cliche comes from, "The way to a man's heart is through his stomach." These days it seems to apply to women just as much.

The mouth is the messenger of love. From birth to old age, the mouth speaks words of endearment, and it is the place we fill with nourishment, which is in itself a loving gesture. There is more to the taste of love than food for the stomach. There is also the taste of a fond, lingering kiss. Our sense of tasting and testing a mate starts with the first kiss.

Soul kissing should be reserved for later when there is trusted fidelity. There are some sex researchers who believe it is possible that under certain circumstances, the HIV virus might be transmitted through saliva. So, play it safe and wait till you are sure. But don't stop kissing. Just do it without saliva and play it absolutely safe. The male tongue placed into the mouth is felt by some women as the first step toward the penis entering the vagina.

The importance of kissing lies in the fact that the lips, the mouth and the tongue comprise an erogenous zone, and whenever erogenous zones are stimulated, the excitation spreads to sexual tissue. Next to the sexual organs, they are the most sensitive parts of the body.

Kiss Your One-and-Only All Over

A kiss can reveal what words conceal. Kissing is the silent language between lovers. How you kiss, how you are kissed in return, and also where you are kissed, can indicate what kind of a sexual relationship to expect from a particular lover. There is no place that should be considered out of bounds, once you have ascertained your sexual health. A clean, healthy body is entirely lovable and kissable.

Reluctance to accept a loved one's body is a sign of inbred inhibition, and may indicate a problem on the part of the reluctant one.

However, where and what one kisses during foreplay is an entirely personal matter and there should be no anxiety about whether one or another kind of kissing is normal or not. Everything is normal if it meets with the approval of both people concerned. No bodily fluids should be exchanged till after tests are taken and until the couple decides to have sex only with each other.

Erotic Ways of Touching

Skin-to-skin contact awakens the most sexual of all the senses. One can close one's eyes, say nothing and let the fingers do the walking and hands do the talking! As they roam over a lover's body, they send exquisite messages of love. The tender emotion in a touch can dissolve all manner of barriers. Touching lets a woman know what sort of man she is getting close to. How eager he is, how tender, how thoughtful, how ardent, how kind.

A lover may not mean the words he is saying, or he can, if he is a skilled actor, look as though he adores you, but the touch of his hands will tell the truth. There are countless ways to touch and be touched - as deep, as high, as wide, as our boundless imagination. It can be a source of comfort and reassurance to the shy or timid. It can be an indication of the best that is yet to come.

The human skin has a massive network of tactile receptors specialized in receiving messages of heat, pain, pleasure, pressure, and so forth. We react in a special way to the soothers, the relaxers of touch. The stroking, massaging, petting of the skin sends a vibration of meaning to the brain and prepares our body for the sexual act. All of the many subtle facets of a person's personality are unconsciously revealed by his/her style of touching.

Each and every part of an individual's body carries with it "touch messages" of that individual's special desires and innermost intentions. Luckily, the spirit of instinctual animalism still survives in the nerves and muscles of our bodies and from this force springs the need to draw closer to someone of the opposite sex. This motivation precipitates the mounting desire for sexual intercourse and its profound closeness. There are countless methods of sensory arousal through the sense of touch. Remember, you should not rush to orgasm. Orgasm is the completion of sexual ecstasy and the build-up is the best part of the experience.

Masturbation- Is it Good or Bad?

A large majority of people were told as children not to touch their "private parts." Today's sex therapists are reversing this notion. They are teaching people that sexual touching is not only permissible, but healthier for singles who might endanger themselves by sleeping-around. For couples, mutual masturbation can remove the walls we build around ourselves. It can protect new lovers from exchanging bodily fluids until they make sure they are both free of HIV and other communicable diseases. Self-stroking to the point of orgasm helps some women overcome repression as well as depression. Many women discover that vibrators help intensify orgasmic feeling and many women who never reached an orgasm find that they can stimulates themselves to the point of climaxing.

When people get into the bad habit of *not* touching (themselves or other people), they tend to dull their perception of pleasure and become alienated from life itself. After you perfect solo masturbation you can graduate to mutual masturbation. Be freely aware of all of nature's wonders, as you enjoy the results of your own touching and the feel of masculinity in contrast to feminine feeling. A woman should run her hands over his buttocks and not miss a spot, get to know every hair and pore of his body. She can then invite him to do the same for her. Women become sensually aroused through participation. *Hint to women:* If your partner is one who becomes overstimulated too quickly, it is sometimes best to direct your needs toward your own arousal.

With practice and experimentation he will become more adept at his own control and be able to cooperate in your further arousal. If he has this problem, direct his attention toward stimulating you. Don't be prudish about it. We only get in life what we ask for, and it is no longer chic to be used by a man as a receptacle in one-sided selfish sex. That's what prostitution is all about, a business for one and pleasure for the other.

Nothing Beats a Good Massage

One of the most effective ways for him to relax and arouse you is through a leisurely, soothing massage. There is tender loving in the art of stroking and manipulation of the body. Massage stimulates and increases circulation. There are as many variations of massage as there are people with creative minds to think them up.

Some people find that a rougher kind of massage excites them more than the soothing style. You might try starting out with the gentle kind of massage and including a few light slaps for the excitement of it. The variations can include everything from a light, gentle tapping of the finger tips, to squeezing and delicate pinching. Some people like to have their backs scratched. Scratching can be very exciting inside the thighs. Nibbling ears can also be stimulating for the receiver as well as the giver. In fact, nibbling any part of the body is allowed and encouraged.

Lovers must communicate their thoughts about this and feel free to ask for what they want and to say no, if that's the way they feel. The sense of touch is dormant in most people. Discover what your own potential is.

A man's warm touch can melt a cold woman, even when her eyes are shut and his lips are silent. A man's touch can tell everything that he wants to say — and sometimes more. It can also give a man's anxiety away. If he is tense, his touch will surely say so. His palms may sweat, a giveaway of tension. There is a vast difference in the feel of a good lover or an unsure one. This is the way that a woman learns what sort of man she is getting close to. A woman can transmit her sexuality through the sureness of her touch.

There are numberless ways of touching and being touched — and so many marvelous places that invite exploration and discovery. The sureness of a lover's touch can give comfort and confidence to the shy or timid person. It can also soothe and calm the highly intense one.

Emotions are reflected in your fingertips. How do they communicate this vibration? The human skin is covered with a massive network of tiny tactile receptors. They are the reviewing stations for bringing outside feeling inside to the central station, the brain. The thinking mind sorts out these impressions and reacts by giving out the appropriate motor responses. Emotional response depends on the type of feeling that is applied to the surface of the skin.

Men also react with relaxed feeling to soothing stroking. When the feeling is pleasant, the nervous system sends pleasurable anticipation to the brain, which relays a signal to "go ahead" and make it better. Once they receive approval, the sexual organs prepare themselves for sexual interaction. However, if there is no approval of the touch of another person, a stop signal flashes and the welcome mat is removed.

Sexual touching starts at the very beginning of outercourse or foreplay, and it is usually the man that initiates the first skin-to-skin contact. This is an established custom in our particular culture, but there is no reason why it should be a rule. For most modern couples it is more enjoyable if they vary the routine and reverse roles. It is very helpful for women to become actively involved, to take the lead and make love in a more assertive manner.

Advice to Women. Don't leave it all up to his mood. Put him in the mood. Show him you want his attention by touching him. Sex always stems from a need to make love to oneself. Being sensually involved with another person presupposes self-acceptance and self-respect. When a woman puts her emotions into motion, the action signals her brain that she is with the action and not just a spectator to the sport. A woman must be encouraged to touch her partner, as well as touch herself. Research confirms that women grow more passionate once they enter the activity.

The old-fashioned custom of a woman just lying there while a man does all the "warming up" is contrary to her own best interests. Non-participation perpetuates lethargy. It is still standard procedure for the male to "prepare the female," to stimulate the flow of her glandular juices. Here is a guide that will accomplish just that (with her cooperation).

Stroking her erogenous zones (throat, ears, nipples, inner thighs, and so on). *Finger manipulation of her clitoris* as well as vulva around opening to the vagina. *Practicing cunnilingus* (when she indicates willingness).

Men deserve special treatment as well. When she runs her fingernails down his back and up his inner thighs, and teases his testicles, he will feel a new kind of excitement. Touch his nipples or any other place that takes him by surprise. This will encourage him to be an adventurous lover and return creative sex-play.

Play the Game of "Touch and Glow." In the erotic game of touching for pleasure, no spot is out of bounds. It's fun when lovers alternate taking the lead, one touching and the other returning the caress. This is a fundamental activity for great outercourse. We call it "Follow the leader." It goes like this:

You tickle her toes, she tickles yours.
You stroke her palm, she strokes yours.
You fondle her hair, and she fondles yours.

And so on, as you play the game of follow the loving leader. Backs get scratched. Thighs get patted. Run your fingertips lightly over the buttocks. Note the variation in texture as you touch each part of each other's bodies. Be aware of the contrast between the male and female skin. Notice the patterns of body hair.

Tips for Men. Cup her hand over your genitals. Then place your hand over her vulva. Quietly observe. Contemplate the wonder of nature's diverse creativity. How wonderfully complimentary our genitals are. Explore with fingers. Don't avoid or miss a spot. Be sure to get to know every pore of her body and invite her to do the same with yours. Notice and enjoy the feel of masculinity in contrasting harmony with her femininity. Guide her to do the same for you.

The caressing nature of massage sets up a special kind of bond between lovers. A married couple, whom I interviewed for this book, mentioned that they have a lot more pleasure out of sex since they have learned how to give each other an erotic massage. He massages her before sexual intercourse, as part of the foreplay, and she returns the favor after they both have their orgasms. She sits on his back and rubs his shoulders and uses her elbows to gently run up and down his spine. When a woman is well prepared before he penetrates her vagina, she has no problem reaching orgasm. Her body wants to do it. When she does, she is so delighted that massaging her husband is a pleasure rather than a chore.

Tips for women. You must open your own doors wide to new dimensions of sensory gratification. You must ask yourself if you are allowing yourself to use all of your senses fully for sexual pleasure — without prudish hangovers from the past. If the answer is no, find out why you are denying yourself your birthright, the pursuit of a most fundamental happiness: the sexual release of mind, body, and emotional tension. The amount of sexual pleasure depends on the degree of sensory awakening.

The Latest Scoop on Condoms

Men must use condoms, unless there is fidelity and no outside cheating. The excuse men give is that sensation is diminished. With mind-control, this is no problem. You can intensify sensation with mind-power. This will also extend staying-power when you train yourself to use a condom properly. Look for the right kind of condom to fit your needs. There are many made in America with additional choices from European and Asian countries. Condoms come in all shapes, colors and sizes. Some even glow in the dark, so you can find what you're looking for. Others are designed with tickling attachments and several women have told me about condoms that are ribbed and actually increase sensation for them internally.

It is possible that some of the newer condoms can improve mutual shared fulfillment, by slowing down orgasm in the man and allowing women more time to respond with penile-vaginal friction. Men can learn to enjoy using condoms.

For men who complain that it lessens their sensation, those in the know suggest you add a drop of KY Jelly, which is water based, to the head of your penis, before putting on the condom. Never use oil-based ointments like Vaseline because oil tends to dissolve the condom. The lubricant restores sensation because it makes the end of the penis slippery against the inside of the condom. Some men say it is an improvement over sex without a condom because it increases friction for the man as well as the woman.

New designs in condoms feature a knob of latex that rides gently up and down against the glans (head) of the penis. One such product is called, "Pleasure Plus." It has been tested at Emory University School of Medicine with 70% of couples reporting satisfaction and preference over any other type.

Another concern about trusting condoms is that they don't always stay in one piece. Some of the old-fashioned types may break because of inadequate lubrication. If there is vaginal dryness, KY Jelly is suggested, or any other water-soluble product.

In putting on the condom it should be rolled up all the way, but not too tight. Leave about one half inch slack at the tip to allow for semen. In taking it off, be careful. Ask the woman for help if necessary. I suggest a couple practice these suggestions until they apply the condom with ease.

To make condom use extremely satisfying, use visualization and positive auto-suggestion during intercourse. Tell yourself, "This feels natural, better and better every time I use it." Combine the suggestion with vaginal squeezes to intensify the sensation.

Chapter 8

Spiritual Sex — Highest Ideal

- ☑ *Bodies and souls united as one*
- ☑ *Cupid, the mythical God of love*
- ☑ *Astral projection during orgasm*
- ☑ *Sexual ecstasy prolonged in time*

 Spiritual intercourse is the kind of union philosopher Johann von Goethe had in mind when he wrote: "The totality which two lovers bring to one another defies calculation. It is infinity, discharged through all eternity." The range of love's ecstasy is boundless. The matching of two bodies and souls is holy in more than an institutional sense: holy in terms of joining a couple's sexual energy with the wholeness of life in the greater universe.

While modern day psychologists do not all agree with everything that Sigmund Freud espoused, his discovery that emotional illness was linked to sexuality, gave us clues that are still valid. He believed the problem with human conflict was dualism, dividing mankind in flesh/body and at the other extreme, mind/ spirit. This breach is the source of great suffering and is responsible for the failure of most human beings to live up to even a modicum of human fulfillments in their lifetimes.

Our senses, trapped in the "good or bad" dichotomy, often turn off our sexual spirit. The tragedy of broken marriages is that these are people who started off loving each other, and just didn't know how to elevate that love to higher unification. When they bored each other to death, the marriage died. The time has come to heal the rift between body and soul. The healthiest intimacy occurs when spirituality blossoms out of free-flowing sensuality as it did with ancient people. Attempts by religious zealots to squelch basic instincts has failed. Many preachers have fallen from grace. We cannot be happy if we divide the body from the spirit. This is what has made so many people emotionally ill in our society.

Body and Spirit Were Once United

The concept of spiritual sex is nothing new. Our ancient ancestors believed in the interaction of sexuality with religious worship. Primitive religions were based on amorous attraction and fertility rites. Great religious sex festivals were held in many types of primitive societies around the world. It may shock some present day prudes, but early human history shows a strong correlation between sexual intercourse and sacred prayer. They often took place simultaneously.

There were many sects that practiced Phallic worship and others that revered the female sex organs as a deity. Long ago, before sexuality and spirituality became antagonists, priests of ancient cultures accepted the close relationship between physical lust and religious fervor. Primitive rituals celebrating sexual readiness attest to the instinctual importance of the total male-female embrace. When lovers embraced each other, they embraced God, as well.

Drums would beat out rhythms, as bodies swayed to sexual vibrations. There was food to please the taste, and pungent oils to tease the libido, with their erotic scents. In all of ancient art, there runs a vein of sexuality, as part of mysticism. Female forms are depicted as equal with the male, and the interplay of psychic and physical sexuality is perceived as a religious phenomenon. Sexuality is apparent in all of religious art and music throughout history. Renaissance paintings on cathedral walls and ceilings depict fleshy bodies, interwoven with the ethereal precepts of the artist. Religious art features physicality. Angels are never sickly and the Cistine Chapel radiates the lusty musculature of the saints.

Sacred Sexual Unification

We see a great deal of sexuality and spirit linked in Eastern religious literature such as the Hindu Ananga Ranga, the guide to love. In it Hindus describe sacred sex this way: "When in such an embrace, your senses are shaken as leaves on a tree. Even the roots are quivering. And a great wind; a great energy is blowing through you; vibrating you; allowing every cell in your body to dance." Genital intimacy is described as the means of apprehending one's divine, higher nature. Blending of the male and female energy has been expressed in countless spiritual and esoteric beliefs: Astrology, Platonism, Taoism, Gnosticism and the ancient teachings of the Kabbalah, to name a few.

Yin-Yang Chinese philosophy calls attention to two basic principles of life: one feminine and the other masculine, as complimentary and necessary to each other. The connection between sex and soul goes back to the earliest religious rituals known to man. Evidence of the practice of worship with procreation exists in ancient cave drawings and prehistoric artifacts. We see in archeology the link between God and sexual intercourse, making it a gift rather than something to be hidden or ashamed of.

In the 5,000-year-old Indian concept of Tantra Yoga, the message is that sex is a sacred experience, because it combines both male and female energies. The acceptance of maleness and femaleness within God is basic to the religious tradition found in Nepal, Tibet, Mongolia, Japan and much of India, where God is a combination of both Devi, (female) and Sheva, (male). The societies touched upon here are a sampling of the broad range of early historical cultures.

However, western religion, as we now know it, came along and decreed that love be divided into two categories and put labels upon each. There is "heavenly" love, and there is the "earthly" kind. Set up as opposing poles of human nature, heavenly has come to mean "sexless" and earthly referred to as "lustful." Heavenly implied high-mindedness and nobility, while earthly love connoted animalism. For centuries sensuality and spiritually have been divided, considered antagonists. This is still a precept of the

Catholic Hierarchy and has been the basic cause of a great deal of emotional distress and mental confusion.

Meet Lusty Eros - God of Love

Sexual passion, often referred to as Eroticism, is named after Eros, God of love. He is said to have exploded like a volcano from the center of earth. With his bright, quivering golden wings, he uttered passionate cries of lust, in an orgastic sexual mating in heaven and on earth. Many offspring have descended from this lusty little creature. Art all over the world is resplendent with chubby-cheeked, winged angels.

Eros, whom we know as Cupid, is displayed on modern valentines as an innocent baby. His sexual fire was cooled down from the original lusty spirit, by Victorian prudes. Today when we see Cupid's sweet, innocent visage, it's hard to imagine that he began as the very hot-blooded, sexual-spiritual God. Homer's classics, *The Iliad* and *The Odyssey* describe Eros as the essence of "irresistible passionate desire." Described as all goodness and light, Eros used the power of his love as an arbitrator of hostilities, between warring nations as well as squabbling humans.

Mythology tells us that Eros fell in love with a beautiful mortal virgin, a princess called, Psyche. Tribute to Psyche's beauty spread far and wide, reaching gods in the heavens as well as mortals on earth. Children scattered flowers at her feet wherever she walked. She could foresee, with her mind, events that others could not. (Psychic insight originated with her, as well as all areas of psychology.)

Cupid, (or Eros) was entranced by all that he had learned about her. However, the gods decreed that Psyche, being mortal, was not fit to marry a god and they were separated. Since that sad moment, the god of love has been searching for his soulmate. Psyche has come to mean the inner connection we all have to our spiritual godliness.

The Heavenly Gift of Spiritual Sex

Once lovers have opened to the arousal of all five senses, the soulmates are ready to merge as one. The full use of all our facilities makes lovemaking much more than a physical activity. Emotions of love bring an ephemeral quality that links the body not only to the mind but to the soul and universal spirit. Soul-mates lift themselves above the mundane stress of living. They refresh and revitalize each other in seclusion, as they retreat from the hectic bustle of everyday life into an ephemeral cloud of renewal. It is a time when they help each other soar from passion's ecstasy to eternal bliss.

Meditation with sensuality opens the door to transcendence that takes you, "out of this world," all the way to a spiritual union. Wisdom throughout the ages has taught us that without the poetic involvement of the spirit, physical attraction is short-lived, but in contrast, spiritual love goes on forever. It helps to comprehend the concept of spiritual sex if you look for a moment at the essential nature of life itself. Biologists know that all living things have one thing in common, whether plant, fish, fowl, or human: regeneration. It comes from joining together parts that are divided. From the tiniest atom to the largest living creature, life expands when two complimentary forces, male and female unite. When opposites join together they create equilibrium and greater balance. This respresents an ideal concept of mating.

The tragedy of haphazard copulation is the absence of unification of spirit and purification that comes with loving devotion. Long-lasting lovers, on the other hand give and receive the gift of the divine embrace, the epitome of all human communication. Any poor soul that gets locked into sex without spirit is missing the best part of loving. They lose the joy of celebration and with it the connection to spirituality. When two bodies become one during spiritual love-making,

At a recent lecture, I spoke to a group of women about relationships. I asked a young woman what message she would like to give to men. Here is her answer, "I would like you to tell them, first of all, that women want to have a deeper connection than just the body. They want men to express their romantic, loving, spiritual nature." Is she expecting too much? I don't think so. I believe that men need spirituality just as much as women do, probably more so.

Men die 10 years sooner than women because they do not know how to exchange sensitive rapport, the kind of interpersonal, empathetic understanding that involves the human soul. Not only do men suffer early death and stress-related disease, but without the spirit factor, marriages and other intimate relationships do not survive. If they do last, they are dysfunctional unions. Long-term fidelity is the highest path to spiritual unity. Mutual desire expands as the erotic excitement spirals upward into the realm of the unknown, spurred by the ebb and flow of love's effervescent vibrations.

If we subscribe to science's belief that time and space have neither beginning nor end, we come face to face with an infinite universe and the concept of eternity. The power of our inner spirit is an expression of infinity. When two souls reach the epitome of sexuality, they feel exhilarated physically and exalted spiritually.

How to Prepare for Spiritual Intercourse

 It helps to create a secluded space without intrusion. Prepare a quiet room with lots of flowers. A scented candle. Wine and fruit. Perfumed bedsheets. Soulful music. All of these help to encourage a deeper union between lovers. Spacing out during lovemaking inevitably leads to an Alpha level of brainwaves, which is an alterred state of mind akin to meditation or light hypnosis. As two bodies merge and become one during sexual intercourse, the couple enter the spectrum of infinite intelligence. On this plane, their souls can touch and greet each other like old friends, comfortably and ego-free.

Once the connection is established between minds, emotions and spirit, threads of empathy and rapport develop between male and female energy. These vibrations are interwoven into a shared pattern and become part of the deepening mutually shared sacred intimacy. The couple loses all earthly anxiety and feels balanced, in harmony with all life in the universe. They do not struggle to reach orgasm nor do they strain to avoid it. They simply flow with the energy passing from one to the other.

Can anyone attain this high level of empathetic intercourse? Maybe not everyone, but certainly so for anyone who is willing to practice the mind-empowering and sensual programs outlined in this book. Remember, it starts with relaxation, deep breathing, imagery and positive affirmative suggestion. All of this happens during foreplay, before penile-vaginal contact. When the penis enters the vagina, a calmness takes over. There is no pressure to succeed or perform.

When you involve all five senses described previously, you will be well on your way to spiritual intimacy. Remember to look into each other's eyes after the sexual organs have connected. This soulful gaze will propel you to enter an alterred state of mind-control that is essential to a spiritual sexual union.

When you develop intimacy of the mind and soul the sexual part becomes more meaningful. Transcending the physical urgency to climax allows time to savor the pleasure of the moment. When this stage is reached, do not be drawn into future expectations or past conditioning, but become fully attuned to the depths of pleasure you feel at a given moment in time. Only then, can two bodies and souls join in unity.

Visualization during sexual intercourse blends the genders into one. What is most spiritual in a virile man is something feminine and what is most spiritual in a feminine woman is something masculine. The senses combine with words of deep affection and appreciation and a profound depth of mutual trust develops. The first step in the astral journey begins with an awareness of living in the here and now. Tell yourself: "Nature has gifted me with all the necessary equipment I need in order to enjoy life on all levels. Embodied in the marvelous structure of my nervous system is the apparatus which enables me to partake of the endless beauty that the universe offers."

Here's How You Get Started

When you attain a level of shared intimacy on a mental, emotional physical level, you are now ready to take the coupling a step further, into the ethereal, spiritual realm. Begin by reclining in a comfortable position along with your lover. Deliberately set aside all conscious thinking about the problems of the day, or the problems of yesterday, or even problems that may occur tomorrow. Think totally in the moment, of the here and now, of how good it feels to release the body of tension. Blend energies with the one you love. Feel the vibrations passing from one to the other. Enjoy scanning each other's face.

Place all thoughts in abeyance. Reject all earthly concerns. Postpone decisions. Leave judgments to a more suitable time. Everything can wait. Take into yourself an inner quietness — a peaceful space, inside your mind. Let your conscious perception of time drift away and just relax all over. Thoughts bring with them the tension of making decisions, so let them float away. Suspend, postpone all judgments. Lay them aside.

As you stroke your lover's body, gaze soulfully into each other's eyes. This brings about a mutually induced trance-like state, akin to hypnosis. Touching as you gaze will bring total arousal, as you drift together into an altered state of mind. Once the eyes have made the connection, let the lips meet, softly. The taste of a kiss can be food for the soul, for it involves not only taste, but touch, smell, and sound as well. Nothing tastes as sweet nor feels as soft as a lover's promising soul-kiss. Kissing is probably the most expressive form of mutual acceptance that is possible. It is the forerunner of total mind-body-spirit involvement.

When lips allow the other to enter, they open doors between people's emotions and minds. The level of sensuality is boosted way up to divine communion. Soul- kissing got its name from the way a man and woman use their mouths to enter into each other. In a committed relationship, soul kissing can include kissing the entire body.

The intangible, spiritual exchange that is experienced in a soul-kiss does more than arouse lovers sexually; it can be the means of assuring one another that they have, indeed, found the mate that fulfills their soul's yearning.

Lovers Share Their Experience

A couple, in their thirties who have perfected this art, told me of the great boost to their health and mental clarity. She said: "When my lover and I are in touch with this power, our joy is limitless. We share this perception as one embodiment of spirit." He said: "Spiritual intercourse gives us  the opportunity to use our sensuality to its fullest degree. We used to have ordinary sex every other night. Now, we are satisfied with less quantity, because the quality is so great."

Enter Your Center of Spiritual Connection

As your lips melt together, problems, like clouds, drift aimlessly by, blown apart by shifting summer winds. Now clouds lose their shape, become wispy, dissolving into the blue of the sky and into the blue of your resting mind. Let all thoughts and ideas pass by as if they belonged to someone else. Don't lay claim to the past. Be in the moment, aware of only one thing: how good it feels to let all accumulated tension go from your body. How delicious it is to luxuriate in a feeling of relaxed restfulness with someone you love sharing a sacred experience, as you drift and shift into another level of being.

Allow yourself to open doors and windows that used to block entrance to your soul and lock the other out. Pierce the mask of any buried hostilities. Let obsolete patterns linked to weaknesses or disappointment dissolve, for they are no longer valid. The past gives way to newborn awareness as old traps are sprung, and imprisoned passion released.

Intercourse continues with very little thrusting or pelvic movement. A stillness takes over as you blend with your love. A warm embrace pervades your soul and entire being. You are one with your mate. Both bodies seem as one. You can roll and slowly shift position without losing the pelvic embrace, or pushing for orgasm. Some lovers have trained themselves to fall asleep in each others arms with the penis inside the vagina. They may awaken hours later or in the morning and continue the love celebration.

Here are a few more descriptions from people who have given up the mundane style of sexual intercourse for this newstyle: "Each time we make love, I learn more about how to respond unselfishly to my mate." "I discovered that sensuality is the gateway to my spirituality." "My body and mind are unified and free from physical restrictions." "I recognize and respect my passionate feelings as something beautiful to share with my lover."

Lovers who experience this joy, learn there is no division between sexuality and spirituality. Here is an exerpt from a letter I received from a woman who had been on the verge of divorce because of boredom and infidelity: "The joy of sexual mating is now an important part of my private life and I regard it as the pathway to reaching my higher self. I have eradicated a lifetime of sexual guilt and see the union of myself and husband as a metaphysical link, both good and godly."

It is a travesty of life that human sex has for centuries been identified as obscene and degrading, performed in shame and dark seclusion. Much of human suffering can be attributed to the fallacious belief that sexual lust is sinful. Lovers who learn to rise above ignorance, stretch the boundaries of human consciousness. It is life's peak ecstasy when a man and woman entwine themselves into one fabric.

Total communication helps us break the mold of past isolation. Most people have felt a gap between moral teachings and the desire for sexual pleasure. To overcome this chasm, lovers need to learn how to heighten and encourage the other's innermost feelings of passion without which any form of spiritual communion could not take place. The role of passion in all religion is meant to open the spirit to a higher source of energy. In the finest relationships of long-lasting love, a couple becomes passionately involved with each other, including mind, body, and soul. Shallow precepts of conformity to traditional limits regarding bodily pleasures are being rejected.

Modern lovers want to be closely linked in every way. This kind of trust establishes the groundwork for ascending to a higher realm during the peak of ecstatic orgasm. When lovers drop their defenses without fear of hurting or being hurt, they draw closer in a spiritual sense as well. Once a person liberates his senses and thinks and acts without self-censure, the mind awakens the sleeping soul. Sexual-spiritual intimacy is governed by a stimulus-response network which calculates how we react to our own sensory messages. For some, the phenomenon becomes metaphysical.

Metaphysical defines the human astral body as a second ethereal self. Buried within each of us, it accompanies us throughout our lifetimes and, many people believe, even survives after death. It is this metaphyisical aspect that is involved in "out-of-body" sexual ecstasy.

Sex as an "Out-Of-Body" Experience

The ultimate response to spiritual sexuality is an out-of-body experience, or *astral projection*. The event takes place when lovers completely discard previous limitations, and allow themselves to become totally focused into the act of love as a personal kind of religious communication. The ability to expand sensory reaction to a spiritual level is triggered by the awareness of a higher consciousness, which we all have, but sometimes lose touch with.

The phenomenon takes place when lovers discard differences and allow themselves to become connected as equals. Two symbiotic halves forming one unit, united with the universe. On this level you will have mastered control of your body's physical function, and also be free of anxiety about performance. This will prepare you to experience a deeper unity, beyond the merging of sexual organs, to the merging of astral souls.

Here's a personal reaction to the experience by a client whose marriage was on the rocks and turned it completely around by adding the spiritual factor:

"I felt a detachment from my body, a strange numbness all over my skin. When I reached orgasm, I lost all sense of conscious awareness. I think I went into some kind of a trance state that was pure bliss. I hated to return to reality because I was experiencing such a beautiful blending with my lover." It is one of the most beautiful rewards of life that when a person gives to another, the giver is also enriched.

"When I touch you, I am touching infinity," said an anonymous poet to his lady-love. Infinity is everywhere - from the myriad of flowers that decorate the earth to the unlimited expansion of the human soul. And nothing is more expansive or spiritual than lovers in total embrace.

Take Time to Ascend to a Higher Plane

Leisurely lovemaking with awareness of living in the moment, starts us in the right direction. Many people live life at a hectic pace, rushing from one place to another, hopping from one lover to the next. This hyper-kenetic lifestyle has also seeped into the way we make love. The rush to reach orgasm stems from the sense that we must quickly get over doing something because it is wrong and we might get caught in the act. We need to radically change attitudes and take plenty of time for lovemaking. The experience should be viewed as a priority activity rather than something sandwiched in between household or watching television. Instead of pushing for the big "O", we need to de-emphasize the climax and enjoy the here and now.

The energy glows and flows throughout every cell and organ of the being, inside and out. Anyone can learn how to slow down and control their sexual reflexes with practice and a new attitude. You will find that the effort is well worth it. You will be cleansed and re-birthed in the deepest sense.

You discovered in Chapter Five, how to enter a state of profound relaxation for positive image meditation. When you have practiced the erotic meditation described in detail there, that will be the threshhold from which you can graduate to spiritual intimacy.

Most people have been indoctrinated with the idea that a spiritual person rises above the needs of the flesh. However, those who do so suffer not only from sexual dysfunction, but emotional instability, as well. We've seen ample proof of this in the tearful outburst of religious evangelists who have strayed from the narrow path of their divided beliefs. They walk a winding road, leading nowhere. People with sensory deprivation have deprived souls and tend to deprive others of loving compassion. Women suffer more than men from guilt and self-doubt. Human beings, considered the wisest of the species, are the only living creature handicapped by sexual dysfunction.

Along with physical problems, many people are sick in spirit, as well. One reason for this widespread malaise is that the unfulfulled body nags the spirit for attention to its biological needs. Only by connecting the spirit to the body can a person overcome malfunction and free both body and soul. The fact that good sex is indispensable to health and spiritual wellness has been amply proven time and again.

Nature's greatest device for keeping a balance in life is the wondrous creation of two opposites that form a complimentary union. Division dissolves as lovers lose selfishness during soulful-sexual intercourse. It is with grandeur that sexual love carries out nature's design for the perpetual continuation of life. Sexual communication can be elevated to the highest peak of godliness when lovers are in accord. To reach this pinnacle of intimacy, men and women must discard "sex for sex's sake," and share higher values. The longing of one's body and soul to blend with another brings us in touch with infinity, based on billions of years of evolution. Bliss-consciousness increases with the repetitive practice of this principle put into action.

Orgasmic embrace symbolize the union of opposites and eliminates the gender gap. As the wheels of ecstasy spin they are linked by the highest creative force that holds everything in this world together, in space and time. The enigma of male to female connection is fully fathomed under this depth of harmony. In contrast, religious propriety has sunken into an immoral division between soul and body and a separation of the sexes. Moral judgments must not be imposed on normal human needs. The epitome of sexuality is to be exalted spiritually. With higher awareness one can sincerely say, "Thank God for sex!," for it is heaven's gift to regenerate the flow of love between mates. Once you have risen above the restrictions of your past, you continuously move toward greater wholeness. Circumstances no longer control your life. You become inner directed and spiritually connected.

Prolonging Orgasmic Ecstasy

A man can learn to distract himself from climaxing by diverting his thoughts from his sexual organ to other points of his body; or better still, to parts of his lover's body. More than merely trying new tricks to intensify orgasm, the mind can also explore creative ways to unite the spiritual core of two lovers and bond them to eternity.

Once you have mastered and control your sexual function you will be free of anxiety about physical performance and be able to move onward and upward to a more meaningful relationship, one that goes beyond the mere physical "getting-together" of sexual organs, into an exchange of spiritual affinity. Out of body projections have powerful therapeutic value, both for those under high stress and for couples who indulge in intercourse simply for pleasure.

After Orgasm — Re-vitalize by Skin Breathing

This is a time to thank each other for this very special experience. Now, lie back with your loved one nestled close to you. Cuddle naked, belly to belly and monitor the vibrations of your combined breathing. Breathe as one entity. Listen to both hearts beating in haromony.

Together, do the following Yoga exercise for enhancing tranquillity to transcend future stress:

First, focus on the surface of your skin.
See your body as a huge, thirsty sponge.
Imagine your skin as eager to soak up air.
Visualize breathing in through your skin.

Breathe out all your stress and tension. Breath is life, and to live fully one must breathe that way. Oxygen circulates energy, and sexual-spiritual gratification demands an extra supply, far above the requirements of normal breathing. With your bodies in close proximity, you should sense each other's pulsations. The slower and deeper you both breathe, the sooner you will synchronize with each other's vibrations. The goal is to blend your inhalations and exhalations until you are both in total harmony. This will take you to the platform of ascendance, where you can rise to an even higher plane of "soul-rapport," the most wonderful reward of a monogamous relationship.

The recent resurgence of marriage and family values carries with it the promise of transforming sexual mediocrity into sublime ecstasy. Sexual intercourse with love becomes a sacred ritual for the lovers who manage to free themselves from guilt and negativity. We can only imagine how blessed children will be born of this kind of heavenly union. Children, conceived in both physical and spiritual devotion, will never need to complain about dysfunctional families.

Cases of Spontaneous Spiritual Intercourse

In rare instances some very sensitive people may have automatic out-of-body experience during sexual intercourse. I have only known this to happen between long-term lovers who have learned to thoroughly relax and trust each other. One woman recalled the happening as: "Ecstacy, indefinitely prolonged," while her mate said it was, "Like an electric shock melted us together. And the closeness has stayed with us."

Group Training in Spiritual Induction

In response to requests from several monogamous couples, I held a special group-therapy to teach advanced techniques of getting into spiritual intercourse. Not everyone who attended thought this an unusual concept. There were a few who had already experienced metaphysical sex without any training. It can happen under highly charged emotional situations. A case in point is that of Delia.

Originally she had come to my office as a teenager, concerned that her parents would discover she was "going steady" with a boy and having occasional sex. When her mother called me to talk about her daughter, it turned out she was fully aware of the young woman's precocious sex drive, but fearful the father would discover his daughter was active sexually.

After several years of intermittent private therapy, Delia, now twenty, joined the therapy group. She told of having been brought up by her parents' strict Middle-Eastern Muslim beliefs. They impressed upon her that an unchaste daughter brings shame to the family. Despite all of the house rules about staying away from boys, Delia had been sexually active since the age of fourteen.

When her parents confronted her, there was a violent argument and she ran away from home. After several years of struggling on the streets she traveled to Canada, where she joined a Yoga Ashram and became a devout member.

There she met a young 'Tantra Yoga' practitioner, and they fell in love. She fantasized the young man as a sort of demi-god, and experienced easy orgasm when she was only fifteen. Induced by strong emotionalism, coupled with a sense of worship, a surge of passion carried them beyond physical intercourse into sharing an "out-of-body experience." Later on, they were able to duplicate the alterred state by first entering a meditative state of consciousness, which they learned in one of my classes.

Delia expanded on her feelings: "My first spaced-out sex really scared me because it happened spontaneously, without my control. A strong force pulled me out of my mind and out of my body. I had never before had sexual intercourse with a man I loved, and it overwhelmed me with its intensity. Even though I wasn't a virgin, this was totally different. We are still together because we know there will never be a different partner for us. It is now four years since Bob and I had our first sex together and it gets better each time. When I reach orgasm I see lights flashing around Bob's head, our bodies are linked together, floating up into the air. Afterward, we have high energy."

Exploration of a New Dimension

They graphically described how heightened loving emotions bring to sex an ephemeral quality. Their unique exploratory lovemaking contributed to the techniques in this book, proving teachers can learn from their students. When a man and woman experience the uniqueness of this kind of intimacy, anything else pales by comparison and there is no chance that such a couple would bother to seek other mates. They are content having brought to each other the ultimate kind of intimacy.

This is obtainable by any couple who will take a little time to train themselves to physically function better, so that they can detach from the body and elevate themselves. This rare event can only take place when lovers completely discard preconceived notions and limitations, accept themselves and each other as blameless and guiltless and therefore worthy of an exalted union. Keep in mind that an altered state of consciousness, through meditation or hypnosis, precedes the "astral" journey.

Another case involved a couple separated by the husband's tour of duty in the Persian Gulf. We have all witnessed or experienced the emotional impact of tearful farewells between lovers. The tender embraces made us realize that one-to-one love is the most important aspect of life. Science tells us that powerful feelings, like the anguish of separation, intensifies the brain's activity. This can lead to a tremendous rush of hormonal response when couples are reunited. The power of sexual-spirit. ' blending is exemplified by the following case: Jack, a twenty-three-year-old, explained how he felt when he was going over seas and had to say goodbye to Cherie. They knew he might never come back and realized how crucial their love for each other was. They had only been married a week before parting.

The three month separation was extremely difficult. They had been the center of each other's lives since grade school. In touch with each other only by mail, and that not too dependable, their longing for each other became so intense that Jack would often experience orgasm merely by reading Cherie's letters. They had many transferences of dream experiences as well.

When the time came that he was finally about to come home to the United States, he telephoned her and they cried together over the good news. Appreciating how precious life was, love for one another was strengthened by longing. Denial of intimacy makes the need grow stronger. It seems swimming against the current, strengthens the soul.

When Jack returned, Cherie was waiting at the airport, and in a state of near hysteria. Within an hour they were in bed, making love. Jack recounted the episode this way: "It was the first time Cherie had been able to experience orgasm without my working real hard to help her. When she knew I was entering the plateau before climaxing, she seemed to flow right along with me into that outward space. It was like taking a trip through the cosmos together."

Cherie added, "It was a heavenly experience, a sensation of soaring or floating above the earth's surface. Our sexual organs seemed to melt together and I didn't know what part was his and what was mine. We gave ourselves to each other, completely." Another person in the training group described the feeling as "liberating, eliminating insecurity. It made my spirit float up through a new dimension of satisfaction." Others made similar statements: "A golden aura seemed to encase both of us like in a religious painting." "It was heavenly! I spaced out of this world." "It was reminiscent of distant stars and unknown galaxies."

Learning to Control the Experience

Jack and Cherie visited my office some months after their first spectacular astral projection. They were disappointed in not being able to achieve the same high as when they made love since that special experience. Participating in the group, they learned the methodology and necessary techniques to repeat the experience. They are, to this day, able to control and improve intercourse up to the level of sacred interaction.

Similar ecstatic ascensions were described by others in the group. A young woman in her late twenties said: "When it happened for me, it seemed like a flash of golden light, instantly over. Then when I looked at the clock, I was shocked to find almost an hour had flashed by. I had lost all sense of time and space."

Many of the others who spoke, mentioned the added pleasure of all six senses being involved. One also described feeling "a new kind of energy being drawn from the collective consciousness of the universe." This is the generic font which is inherent in every human and we are, with self-training, capable of tapping the source.

When we involve all sensory perceptors, sensation is not relegated to the genitals alone, it is spread throughout all the body. Not only does it reach the erogenous zones, like throat, breasts, inner thighs, ears and mouth, but it extends from the fingers to the tips of the toes. The total joy of sex and spirit are joined as one. After entering your spiritual center, establish eye rapport and share breathing rhythms. Here is a sampling of the feelings that flow from one lover to the other: "Our bodies are joined as one now, we float in a cloud of golden light. We are exchanging strength and energy of infinity. There is no time or space. We identify with the source from which all wonders flow. Our sexual organs are uniting our souls. There is a "raying-out" from the infinite mind. I give to you my true sexual identity, male amd female, which is partly you and partly me. I will give of myself whatever it is you need and feel free to take from you, the same. Your vital energies flow into my body, cleansing healing and nourishing. I return them to you enriched with my everlasting love. My sexual organs scintillate in answer to your vibrations." It is not necessary to speak out about love. Feel the attunement in silence as you emerse yourself in sensation, which includes spirituality plus sensuality.

Although science tells us that altered consciousness is triggered by brain chemicals, experience has taught me that we can produce this trigger through self-empowerment and suggestion. Energy is essential to assure that the brain will be excited into manufacturing these necessary chemicals for each stage of our sexual fulfillment — from infatuation to spiritual exaltation.

Shared love is indispensable as a state of receptivity to higher consciousness. Only when the body's needs are satisfied can the spirit really free itself. It is strange that man, supposedly the more liberated of the sexes, is still handicapped by sexual dysfunction and, very often sick in spirit.

Many men have difficulty in practicing spiritual sex because they do not accept and love their own feminine side. Research points to the possibility that the sharp division of the sexes has caused men to disassociate from their spiritual nature. Many men are divided within. They have attempted to bury their true androgynous nature.

Gender Contrast is Spiritual

Ancient paintings and sculpture depict God as possessing both male and female sexual organs. In more modern times, the Swiss psychiatrist Carl Gustav Jung (1875-1961), updated this ancient concepts. He asserted that strong sexual attraction becomes spiritual when a man projects his higher self onto a woman, and vice versa. The male's "Anima" (feminine hidden self) is attracted to the signs of her own masculinity, "Animus," in herself. Mutual acceptance of each other's contrasting nature increases the understanding between the sexes. Allowing the softer side of man's nature to flourish could protect him against breaking down when he faces the many stresses of life. Women have to be willing to accept the softer side of men just as men need to enjoy women's new found assertiveness.

The widespread sexual violence, which has escalated to unbelievable proportions, can be linked to the absence of spirituality in the way most men view sexual intercourse. Ninety thousand cases of rape against women are perpetrated in the United States during a single year. It's been estimated by professionals that only one out of ten cases of sexual violence is ever reported because of humiliation and shame. The true figure of rape and abuse against mainly women and children may be astronomical.

Spiritually minded people do not use sex for releasing hostility. The man who accepts the female within himself perceives sex as the extension of love. When the concept of divine intercourse is accepted, negative behavior tends to be diminished. Sex loses its animalistic projection and is replaced by divine communion. Reaching this kind of blissful high is impossible in casual encounters. It takes investing time and devotion in order that we learn everything about the other person's true nature, to wipe out separation and divisiveness.

People who attain the acme of intimacy become masters of their own destiny and are able to eliminate gender antagonism and blend with the opposite gender to complete nature's cycle.

Conclusion

It behooves men to take a fresh look at women as peers instead of second-rate people. The elimination of exploitation of one another, combined with cooperative communication can bring reality to our dreams of shared happiness. We can direct and control the condition of the earth and the small piece that dwells in each of us. We can apply our power to make the human family equal and mutually helpful, spreading good-will around the planet, bringing the greatest good for the greatest number. We have at our disposal today assets that, if used, can make the world of the 21 century a thing of beauty and nobility beyond the dreams of the prophets and ancient seers who had little knowledge and no technology with which to build the world of their dreams. Let's do it.

Man's nature is not a fixed entity, but is highly flexible with potential of expanding and actualizing his inate creative talents. Possibilities far exceed any yet reached. Man is no longer a victim of nature. On the contrary he has victimized nature. In spite of the size of his brain, man has destroyed the eco system of his body as well as the earth which strives to nourish him. When he learns how to use his intellgience in a constructive manner, man will not only heal himself, but the environment, as well. It begins with loving himself and extended that feeling toward his mate.

Spirit, as well as sexuality are forces present in every person, from birth until death. Our limitless creativity can escalate sex to the epitome of exhilaration that comes when two beings dissolve into one and form a perfect wedding of body and soul. Mutual involvement in the process of expanding sensory feelings opens the avenues to higher consciousness. Lovers are cleansed through the religious feeling of becoming "one flesh." When this kind of closeness is enjoyed there can be no monotony in monogamy.

The ascension begins when lovers intensify all of their means of communication — sight, hearing, smell taste, and touch, to become so close that they meld and merge. At this point, the mind carries them away from their bodies to an exalted space outside of themselves. It is during the genital embrace that we truly become one with the cosmos and readily understand why they say: "Perhaps there is no sex in heaven, because our sexual heaven is here and now."

With this kind of intimate exploration, boredom is impossible, and infidelity inconceivable. Each partner becomes a new person to the other with each rebirthing experience because sexual-spiritual intimacy makes one feel born again. The first prerequisite is respect for the physical body: "A healthy body is the chamber of the soul," was first said by Hippocrates, father of medicine, in 400 B.C. Its wisdom is just as true today.

We can choose between treating the body as a temple of love or as a sewer to dump waste and toxins. Unfortunately, too many people treat their bodies in a hurtful manner. A couple who desires spiritual union should be aware that they must first optimize physical health. This includes what they do and what they don't do. Proper nutrition, ample exercise and freedom from addictive habits, such as alcohol, drugs and tobacco, all are necessary for sharing a higher consciousness. High-minded lovers need no outside stimulant to make them feel "high." They just need each other.

True lovers become experts at turning each other onward and upward instead of going down-hill in mutual degradation. They escort each other on a trip to cloud nine. And when they reach this exalted position they can continue far beyond, developing their own style of astral experience. Because of the violence and conflict going on in the world today, we must open up to new pathways of love, as well as re-examine the wisdom of ancient ways of keeping peace. There is a continuom of life, from the first cell animal to the highest example of intelligence, the human being. It is up to us to encourage cooperation and affection not only between individuals but also between races and nations. It all begins when two people expand their loving feeling and radiate its benefits all around them. Love is contagious. We can all join together to spread warm waves of love all around the globe.

Let's hope we all learn to use our intelligence for higher purposes than human beings seem to be doing. Instead of struggling for power over one another, it's time to call upon the power of love to heal the conflicts in marriage and in every sphere of humanity. Love is the validator. And, above all, love is time-binding. It carries us from one stage of life to the next, and from one generation to another. It can unite the world into one people.

Spiritual love has the power to spread from individuals to everyone they come in contact with and then from one nation to another and affect the entire universe. *Let's help it happen by loving one another unconditionally.*

About The Author

A featured speaker at the 1995 World Congress of Sexology, Rachel Copelan, Ph.D., is the "sexpert" of the 90s.

Dr. Copelan has authored several other best-selling books on sexuality and hypnotism, including *The Sexually Fulfilled Woman* (featured in *Playgirl*), *The Sexually Fulfilled Man* (featured in *Playboy*) and *How to Hypnotize Yourself and Others*. Her works have been published in over a dozen languages.

Dr. Copelan is an internationally respected Marriage Counselor and Sex Therapist, as well as a columnist, author and lecturer. She is an active member of MENSA, an international society for people with high I.Q.

Dr. Copelan has appeared on all major television and radio talk-shows. She resides in Los Angeles, California.